The Homeowner's Guide to For Sale By Owner

Everything You Need to Know to Sell Your Home Yourself and Save Thousands

— with Companion CD —

Revised 2nd Edition

By: Jackie Bondanza
Revised by: Jim Kim
Foreword by: John R. Thomas, Certified Mortgage Planner

THE HOMEOWNER'S GUIDE TO FOR SALE BY OWNER: EVERYTHING YOU NEED TO KNOW TO SELL YOUR HOME YOURSELF AND SAVE THOUSANDS — WITH COMPANION CD REVISED 2ND EDITION

Copyright © 2016 Atlantic Publishing Group, Inc.
1405 SW 6th Avenue • Ocala, Florida 34471 • Phone 800-814-1132 • Fax 352-622-1875
Website: www.atlantic-pub.com • Email: sales@atlantic-pub.com
SAN Number: 268-1250

Library of Congress Cataloging-in-Publication Data

Names: Bondanza, Jackie, 1980- author.
Title: The homeowner's guide to for sale by owner : everything you need to
  know to sell your home yourself and save thousands / by Jackie Bondanza.
Description: 2 Edition. | Ocala : Atlantic Publishing Group, Inc., 2016. |
  Revised edition of the author's The homeowner's guide to for sale by
  owner, 2010. | Includes bibliographical references and index.
Identifiers: LCCN 2016034052 (print) | LCCN 2016043444 (ebook) | ISBN
  9781620230688 (alk. paper) | ISBN 1620230682 (alk. paper) | ISBN
  9781620230848 (ebook)
Subjects: LCSH: House selling--Handbooks, manuals, etc. | House
  selling--United States--Handbooks, manuals, etc.
Classification: LCC HD259 .B65 2016 (print) | LCC HD259 (ebook) | DDC
  643/.120973--dc23
LC record available at https://lccn.loc.gov/2016034052

Printed on Recycled Paper

Printed in the United States

INTERIOR LAYOUT: Antoinette D'Amore • addesign@videotron.ca
COVER DESIGN: Meg Buchner • meg@megbuchner.com

Reduce. Reuse.
RECYCLE.

A decade ago, Atlantic Publishing signed the Green Press Initiative. These guidelines promote environmentally friendly practices, such as using recycled stock and vegetable-based inks, avoiding waste, choosing energy-efficient resources, and promoting a no-pulping policy. We now use 100-percent recycled stock on all our books. The results: in one year, switching to post-consumer recycled stock saved 24 mature trees, 5,000 gallons of water, the equivalent of the total energy used for one home in a year, and the equivalent of the greenhouse gases from one car driven for a year.

Over the years, we have adopted a number of dogs from rescues and shelters. First there was Bear and after he passed, Ginger and Scout. Now, we have Kira, another rescue. They have brought immense joy and love not just into our lives, but into the lives of all who met them.

We want you to know a portion of the profits of this book will be donated in Bear, Ginger and Scout's memory to local animal shelters, parks, conservation organizations, and other individuals and nonprofit organizations in need of assistance.

— Douglas & Sherri Brown,
President & Vice-President of Atlantic Publishing

Table of Contents

Foreword

The rules of the real estate game have changed since the mortgage meltdown of 2007. Selling your home today is completely different than it was back then, because the market has rebounded with vigor. In many areas, home prices have returned to pre-meltdown levels. In other areas, home prices have soared to new highs. If you want to be successful at selling your home for the highest price possible, follow the advice outlined in this book. Jackie Bondanza has written an updated guide to selling your home yourself — commonly called "For Sale By Owner."

Times have changed. We've moved from a buyer's market to a seller's market, which is good news for you. But selling a home by owner is not without challenges, even when market trends are shifting in your favor. You need updated methods and sound advice. This book will guide you through the process from start to finish.

Start by understanding the current housing market. In chapter 1, Bondanza discusses the history of housing over the last 25 years, including the real estate crash in the Great Recession of 2008–2009, which laid the foundation for today's thriving market.

With the proper tools and education, you can save thousands of dollars and control the whole transaction from start to finish. This book will also guide you in knowing which professionals you can partner with for free to help you market and sell your home.

You will find case studies from industry professionals in each area of the book. These will add insight from people working in the field every day. You also receive a CD-ROM with all the needed legal forms to sell your house. The information contained on the CD-ROM could cost you hundreds of dollars and much time to get all the correct and updated forms.

As a Certified Mortgage Planner and Branch Manager for Primary Residential Mortgage, Inc. in Newark, Delaware, I found this book to be a serious step-by-step guide for how to sell your house. I work with For Sale By Owners in Delaware and Maryland to help them sell their homes quickly and for the highest price possible. It took me years to learn half of the information contained in Bondanza's book. I now recommend all of the FSBOs who contact me to get a copy of this book.

The *Home Owners Guide to For Sale By Owner* is your complete handbook that will take you from "For Sale" to "Sold."

John R. Thomas, BA, MEd Certified Mortgage Planner
Primary Residential Mortgage, Inc.
www.DelawareMortgageLoans.net

Introduction

Regardless of how you sell your house, where it is located, or what kind of market it is, selling your house is a big task that requires a significant investment in time, patience, research, and quite often, money. Optimizing the amount of profit you receive from the sale is the ultimate goal, which is why the concept of selling your own home versus enlisting the services of a real estate agent is so enticing.

By definition, "For Sale by Owner," or "FSBO," is the process of listing a property on the market and selling it without the use of a real estate agent to represent that property. Real estate agents serve the purpose of representing properties to potential buyers and managing the sales process, which includes advertising, marketing, hosting open houses and private showings, negotiating, drafting and advising on contracts and other required paperwork, and coordinating the closing process. An agent's job, in general, is to act on behalf of a seller to oversee the selling process and manage all communication on behalf of the seller.

The concept of buying and selling real estate has existed for centuries, as people learned the value of trading land. The role of the real estate agent evolved out of this concept and organized associations of real estate agents dates back more than a century. In 1908, the National Association of Realtors was founded. It later changed to The National Association of Real Estate Boards in 1916, then finally the National Association of Realtors in 1972. The association has since grown to include hundreds, if not thousands, of local chapters for each community across the country.

Like many careers, the role of the real estate agent has shifted and evolved with time. Although agents are required to be licensed and to pass a series of tests to become an agent, some agents are not qualified to effectively handle the process of selling your house on your behalf. This is one of the main reasons homeowners choose to sell on their own as opposed to listing their houses with a real estate agent.

Other reasons FSBO sellers choose to sell on their own include a desire to save the commission fee for an agent. Some sellers will choose to offer a commission to any real estate agent who brings in a buyer. Yet others will enlist the services of a discount brokerage or similar service to aid them in one particular part of the selling process.

Whatever your intentions for deciding to sell FSBO, *The Homeowner's Guide to For Sale by Owner: Everything You Need to Know to Sell Your Home on Your Own and Save Thousands* and the accompanying CD-ROM will take you through all the necessary steps to successfully sell your house on your own. This easy-to-read guide will provide you with crucial, detailed information on preparing your home for sale, listing your home, marketing and advertising your home, creating a comparative market analysis to determine a listing price, dealing with buyer's real estate agents, gauging the market in your local community, and enticing buyers.

The chapters in the book follow the process of selling your house as it would naturally unfold. The book begins with a history of the real estate market, including a look at the housing market crash of 2008 and the subsequent recovery. It ends with valuable information about the closing process and pitfalls to avoid. The CD-ROM includes all the necessary common real estate forms you will need along the way, downloadable with the click of your mouse.

In addition, *The Homeowner's Guide to For Sale by Owner* outlines specific instructions on how to draft a contract that protects your interests, what contingencies to include, how to offer seller concessions, and what to do if your home is not selling. This book will also discuss using discount brokerages and other services to help you sell. It presents the pros and cons of selling FSBO, which can help you determine if FSBO is for you.

With so much information available on the Internet, and so many websites and companies targeting FSBOs, it is imperative you have the right information to make informed decisions during the home-selling process. There are many people, mostly professionals in the real estate industry, who will attempt to discourage any seller from selling FSBO — these are mostly real estate agents who want listings. After all, this is how they make their money. Others, like real estate attorneys, have seen the legal ramifications of the uninformed seller who does not include any protective clauses in his contract and ends up losing thousands in a sale that goes bad.

The reality is, selling FSBO can be extremely profitable and could potentially save you thousands of dollars *if* you are smart about how you go about the process and if you are an informed homeowner. You must be willing to invest the necessary amount of time and research to make the process as smooth, convenient, and beneficial for all parties involved as it can be.

FSBO is not for everyone, but *The Homeowner's Guide to For Sale by Owner* demonstrates just how easy and profitable it can be to sell your home on your own. Good luck!

Chapter 1

What You Should Know Before You Go FSBO

Before you decide to sell on your own instead of listing your house with a real estate agent, there are many factors to consider. Do you have the time to host open houses and devise a marketing strategy? How about creating fact sheets and taking pictures of your house to include in your online listing? Are you familiar with contracts and comfortable negotiating with buyers? This chapter is dedicated to a discussion of these issues and to weighing the pros and cons of selling your house on your own.

Understanding the Real Estate Market

The laws of supply and demand govern the real estate market, like anything available for purchase. Naturally, if there is plenty of supply and not as much demand, prices will be lower. If there is a high demand for a product and it is in short supply, prices will be higher.

When demand and prices are high, the market is referred to as a seller's market because the seller has a product that is in demand and therefore holds more of the power than a buyer does. In the opposite kind of market, a buyer's market, the buyer holds the power because demand is much lower and sellers are at the mercy of the demand, or the buyers. After the housing market crash of 2008, most areas of the nation became a buyer's market because so many homeowners were forced to sell their house as a result of financial issues that were caused by the housing and mortgage crisis. Subsequently, the real estate market embarked on a slow but sustained recovery that led to buyer's markets in many areas.

Trends in the market

In order to grasp where your house stands in the big housing picture, it is important to research and understand the real estate market on a national as well as a local level.

On a national level, the housing market has changed dramatically since late 2008 as a result of the recession and recovery.

During the early 2000s, real estate sales boomed as the government slashed interest rates and banks and mortgage lenders made it very easy for buyers to obtain mortgages. According to *The Boom and the Bust of the U.S. Real Estate Market: What Went Wrong and the Lessons We Learned* by David S. Bunton of the Appraisal Foundation, there have been two real estate booms in the past century: the first following World War II, and the second between 2000 and 2006. The housing collapse of the 1980s and early 1990s deserves mention as well as one of the more significant time periods for real estate.

The first housing boom following World War II was stimulated when thousands of people returned from war in the hopes of pursuing the American dream and buying a home. The number of homeowners across the United States has steadily grown since this boom many decades ago, and the percentage of people who own their own home peaked at nearly 75 percent just before the housing market soured beginning in 2007.

In the decades following World War II, the real estate market hit peaks and valleys but remained relatively steady until the 1980s, when the market took a steep nosedive. During the early part of this decade, many economical factors began to change that contributed, at least in part, to the downturn in the real estate market. First, demand for commercial real estate for business and commercial development led to overdevelopment in many areas of the country, leaving many investors and developers unable to recover funds. Secondly, under then-President Ronald Reagan, small businesses boomed prior to this era as more Americans invested money in starting their own business. When many of these businesses failed, owners who had invested the majority of their personal finances and property in the business lost everything, including their homes, thus pushing foreclosure rates to triple during this time.

In addition to business failings, declining home values due to a lower inflation rate also contributed to the foreclosure rate. In the years leading up to the 1980s, inflation drove up the value of real estate across the board. The Federal Reserve, the arm of the government that regulates the banking system, had minimized the high inflation rates of the previous decade, which ultimately led to decreased home values. Credit card use also began to rise during this decade as more and more homeowners used more credit and saved less. Another contributing factor to the housing market collapse of the 1980s was the de-regulation that large businesses, corporations, and banks enjoyed during Reagan's presidency. Since these businesses were not held accountable to the government in many ways, consumers were much less protected.

Perhaps the most significant catalyst for the housing collapse of the 1980s was the failure of the Savings and Loan (S&L) institutions to provide loans and mortgages to the public. Savings and Loans institutions were banks that offered low-interest loans that were FDIC-insured. The Federal Deposit Insurance Corporation, or the FDIC, is an agency established by the federal government to insure money in national banks and other financial institutions. During the early 1980s, the government eased restrictions and requirements on loan while allowing S&Ls to raise interest rates, which resulted in tremendous growth of these institutions over the following years as they gave out loans to real estate investors and businesses. By the mid-1980s, S&Ls began to level off and fail as a result of bad loans and by 1989 the entire industry needed a bailout. The government passed the Financial Institutions Reform, Recovery, and Enforcement Act when it ran out of money to insure loans made by S&Ls.

The problems the real estate market saw in the 1980s followed into the next decade. During the early 1990s, the availability of credit was severely diminished for those wishing to buy a home. As budget deficits increased, the country was forced into an economic recession. In the early 1990s, new home construction fell to the lowest it had been in decades.

The pre-2007 market boom

It took nearly the entire decade of the 1990s for the housing market to bounce back, which led to the boom that began in 2000. From 2000 to 2006, home purchases boomed across the country as prices in many areas like Florida, California, and Las Vegas more than doubled.

Demand was high during this time mostly because getting a loan was very easy and interest rates were at record lows. While the 1980s saw interest rates soar above 15 percent, interest rates were as low as 5 percent by 2000. Banks began lending money to people who were not qualified for a loan under traditional loan requirements through the use of a subprime mortgage. Guidelines on prime loans were loosened, and still others who did not qualify for prime loans began taking out subprime mortgages.

A subprime mortgage is a mortgage created for an individual who is not an ideal candidate for a "prime" loan. These individuals may have had bad credit, significant debt, or not enough income to qualify for a loan. Because banks could not offer prime loans to these individuals, they began offering subprime loans that sometimes came with steep, adjustable interest rates. The borrower had the option of fixed or adjustable rates. For the first few years of the mortgage, the borrower could enjoy reasonable interest rates after which the rate could be adjusted and inflated to meet the market value.

Other forms of subprime loans enabled borrowers to pay only the interest they owed on the loan for a specified amount of time, usually five to ten years, after which the borrower was required to pay the entire remaining balance of the loan. This type of loan is referred to as a balloon loan.

What is the difference between a mortgage broker and a mortgage lender?

A mortgage lender is a bank or credit institution that lends money to individuals. A mortgage broker works for a variety of different lenders as a middleman to sell loans to individuals.

Traditionally, banks packaged a group of mortgages together and re-sold these mortgages to the secondary mortgage market, which included institutions like Freddie Mac and Fannie Mae. These institutions paid banks for the loans, which freed up funds so banks could give out more loans to more individuals. During 2000 to 2006, banks went beyond selling these loans to just institutions like Freddie Mac and Fannie Mae, and sold them to banks and other financial institutions like Citibank. In order to create a higher return on investment (ROI) on these loans, lenders sold many subprime loans to these other financial institutions, who then became the "owners" of these loans and therefore the beneficiaries of the interest they produced. The debt obligation of these loans taken on by larger banks on Wall Street is known as a mortgage-backed security. The problem was that subprime loans should have been rated accordingly so investors were aware of what they were buying. The risk would have been managed much differently.

What is a Mortgage-Backed Security?

According to the U.S. Securities and Exchanges Commission, "Mortgage-backed securities (MBS) are debt obligations that represent claims to the cash flows from pools of mortgage loans, most commonly on residential property. Mortgage loans are purchased from banks, mortgage companies, and other originators and then assembled into pools by a governmental, quasi-governmental, or private entity. The entity then issues securities that represent claims on the principal and interest payments made by borrowers on the loans in the pool, a process known as securitization."

When these financial institutions demonstrated significant interest in purchasing these loans, they provided lenders with even more incentive to grant subprime loans to more and more people. As a result, restrictions and qualifications were considered even less as lenders peddled faster to churn out more subprime loans to sell. Since mortgage companies were simply going to grant a loan and then turn around and re-sell it, thus passing the assets and the debt off to another company, they had no reason to make sure the loans were given to people who could afford them.

By the 2007, home values began to decrease while interest rates rose for those with adjustable rates, which greatly increased monthly payments. As more people were forced to foreclose on their homes because they could afford their mortgage payment — after all, they were never able to afford the mortgage in the first place — the effect rippled through the owners of these defaulted loans: banks on Wall Street. The banks on Wall Street that purchased these loans were stuck with loans that were not being repaid, and the banks were left with the loss.

According to Barry Wardell, Senior Vice President of Franchise Operations for Assist-2-Sell, a discount brokerage with offices across the country, the housing market crash can be simplified to this explanation: Inventory, or the number of homes on the market, grew when people saw they should sell, then buyers saw they could wait to purchase. "With too many homes on the market, buyers get nervous, and then there is too much inventory," Wardell said.

The crash of 2008

The housing market crash of 2008 affected every market across the country in some way.

Each city and town was affected differently depending on the nature of the local market. Although prices leveled off or fell drastically in many places, many experienced nothing more than stabilization of pricing and others only small declines in the median house price. In cities like Houston and San Antonio, for example, the housing market did not see a drastic change in comparison to some other cities and states because of the nature of the local market: unemployment remained relatively low in comparison to other cities, and the median house price remained relatively stable. Other Midwestern cities saw similar results, while coastal states like California and Florida have seen terrible foreclosure rates.

On the other hand, people in areas like Las Vegas saw rapid development in the years leading up to the crash when the market was booming. The market crash forced many developers to abandon their construction and to take significant hits on any profits from selling these houses because there was so much supply and not enough demand. High unemployment rates and a sharp decrease in house values due to overdevelopment contributed to the condition of the market after the housing market crash.

In states including California, Nevada, and Florida, housing prices rose more than 90 percent during the economic boom in the first half of the decade, which played a significant role in the decline during the recession. "What goes up fast, comes down hard," said real estate author Walter Hall. Because of overdevelopment and the rapid pace of new construction in areas like Las Vegas, these markets are the ones hit the hardest because of the excess of housing, referred to as "inventory" by many industry professionals.

The national average of unsold inventory, which is homes on the market (expressed in months), fell to 3.9 months in early 2016, according to the National Association of Realtors. That's the lowest figure since January 2005, reflecting tightening supply across the country. Unsold inventory indicates how quickly homes are being bought across the country. The index indicates the amount of time it will take for all the homes on the market, the inventory, to sell. The lower the amount of time, the healthier the market.

State of the current real estate market

The Great Recession lasted from December 2007 until June 2009. Since then, the economy has improved, often in fits and starts. While the overall economic recovery has been somewhat lukewarm, the recovery in the real estate market has been anything but tepid. Real estate prices rebounded in many areas of the country. In many areas, real estate prices soared to record heights. In some of the most active markets — San Francisco, Seattle, and others — there's a lot of talk that another real estate bubble is forming.

Sellers, of course, sense opportunity. They now have the upper hand. Buyers, on the other hand, have felt compelled to resort to increasingly aggressive tactics. *Forbes* noted one fairly typical example in Oakland. A prospective buyer of a house listed for $699,000 was confident that the seller would receive multiple offers, many of which would likely exceed the listing price. So the buyer went all-out, offering $200,000 above the listing price with no contingencies. She also submitted a personal letter "describing the multiple generations of her long-time Californian family who would eventually benefit if she bought the home."

The buyer ended up beating out 11 other suitors. Whew! "Honestly, I thought it was a complete long shot. With that much competition, you couldn't tell how crazy the prices were going to go. I feel like we scored!" she told *Forbes*. "That's crazy to say. Two hundred thousand over asking price and I quote 'I feel like we scored!'"

Research from Redfin, the nationwide real estate brokerage, makes it clear that such frenzied activity is not limited to a few large, upscale metropolitan markets. Mid-range homes have powered the recent real estate market in many areas. In the market for homes valued at $200,000 to $400,000, 55 percent of offers by Redfin agents faced some form of competition in March 2016. For homes in the $400,000 to $800,000 range, 60 percent of offers faced competition. In the market for homes valued at $1.5 million or more, 46 percent of offers faced bidding wars or multiple bids. Overall, the percentage of homes for which bidding wars broke out stood at 59 percent in March 2016 — clearly indicative of an active market.

Another telling trend is that the supply of homes is dwindling. "America is experiencing a housing shortage. Not only are there fewer homes available to buyers of all income levels, those just starting out or making their first foray into home ownership are worse off than they've been in years. There are fewer homes available, and even if they can find a home, it's likely to be more expensive," according to a report from Ralph McLaughlin, chief economist at Trulia.

Trulia data segments the market into three tiers: Starter homes, trade-up homes, and premium homes. In all three segments, supply is tightening, helping to drive prices higher.

Starter home inventory has declined the most, falling 43.6 percent from 2012 to 2016. At the same time, the percentage of starter homes of all homes dropped from 30.2 percent to 27.7 percent. Trade-up home inventory has also declined, falling 41 percent from 2012 to 2016. The percentage of trade-up homes fell from 27.2 percent to 26.1 percent. And the inventory of premium homes on the market fell 33.4 percent, while the share of such homes rose 42.7 percent to 46.2 percent.

"Why is inventory so low, especially for starter and trade-up homes? Three reasons: First, investors bought many of the foreclosed homes during the recession and turned into rentals. Second, a larger share of lower-priced are homes are still underwater compared to premium homes, which means that these homeowners are unlikely to sell and take a loss. Third, and most importantly, rising prices are creating homebuyer gridlock. In other words, the spread of homes prices, specifically the growing difference between premium homes prices and trade-up home prices, is likely causing a decrease in trade-up home inventory," according to McLaughlin's report.

While the real estate boom has been felt across the country, the hottest markets seem to be near regional high-tech centers, notably Silicon Valley. Realtor.com offered a list as of June 2016 noting the hottest markets:

1. Vallejo, CA	11. Columbus, OH
2. San Francisco, CA	12. Detroit, MI
3. Dallas, TX	13. San Jose, CA
4. Stockton, CA	14. Kennewick, MA
5. San Diego, CA	15. Santa Cruz, CA
6. Santa Rosa, CA	16. Eureka, CA
7. Denver, CO	17. Ann Arbor, MI
8. Sacramento, CA	18. Grand Rapids, MI
9. Modesto, CA	19. Boston, MA
10. Fort Wayne, IN	20. Los Angeles, CA

As of the summer of 2016, many were predicting that the real estate market nationwide was due for a cooling-off period, which, of course, wouldn't be surprising after such a tremendous run-up.

The market continues to change, evolve, and improve on a daily basis. It is essential to understand not only the current condition of your local market, but also what the future looks like. Conducting research on websites like Trulia (**www.trulia.com**) and Zillow, two leading online real estate platform that provides extensive information on real estate, is a solid idea. *Forbes* magazine is also an excellent source for real estate information, and media like the *New York Times* and *Business Week* are excellent sources for in-depth coverage of the national market.

What today's market means for you

If you are selling a house in an area that is attractive for first-time buyers especially, you have an advantage. This is very market-specific; houses around $150,000 or less are typically houses that first-time buyers are attracted to, because they can afford them. Another significant incentive to purchase a house is the availability of Federal Housing Administration (FHA) and other government loans and grants. More information is available at the Department of Housing and Urban Development website: **www.hud.gov**. Keeping this in mind, you can target your marketing to locations, businesses, and areas where younger, first-time buyers may live or be employed.

The government remains active in aiding first-time buyers, so this group of buyers is somewhat of an exception to the rule simply because they have another option for financing that others who do not fall into this category do not have. Recent changes to government programs make it less costly for some first-time buyers to afford a down payment and private mortgage insurance.

For example, thanks to a recent federal rule change, the premium that people with FHA-backed loans must pay for mortgage insurance was recently cut to 0.85 percent from 1.35 percent. Because of that change, the average homebuyer could save $900 a year.

In addition, Fannie Mae and Freddie Mac — which purchase home loans from lenders and then bundle them for resale to institutional investors — were planning to adopt new guidelines on down payments. The net effect of these changes would be that borrowers would be able to buy a home with a down payment as low as 3 percent, down from 5 percent.

To learn more about FHA and other types of government loans and grants, visit **www.hud.gov,** the U.S. Department of Housing and Urban Development website. The site provides detailed information on FHA and other government loans, news and updates on the status of the housing market, and tips and tools for homeowners to avoid foreclosure.

"Chasing the market" is a term used to describe the act of entering a market after a trend has already passed. In terms of the housing market, this could mean listing a home above its value when the market has begun to take a downturn and prices for similar homes are lower. A seller in this situation would likely be forced to reduce his price to attract buyers, perhaps more than once, which is referred to as "chasing the market." The key to selling quickly is to get in front of the market by pricing your home slightly below market value, for example, instead of pricing above it and being forced to reduce.

CASE STUDY: "IT WAS ALL EASY"

Tina Hill
Successful FSBO seller

In 2004, Tina Hill had the ideal FSBO sale. She decided to sell her home in Massachusetts on her own, without the help of any real estate professional, and set out to do just that. In 2004, the market was booming and Hill took full advantage of the potential she saw. "We listed our house for $950,000 and got the asking price the same day at our one and only open house at 6 p.m. that night," she said.

From the day Hill put the "For Sale" sign in her front yard to the day she closed the entire process took only one month, which is the ideal amount of time to have a home on the market. Hill found the entire process very easy, manageable, and smooth, and she did not experience any significant complications. "It was pretty easy and went smoothly but getting all my home repairs done in time for the open house was my only worry," she said.

As for the home repairs, one of the most important things to take care of before listing your home, Hill had only some minor work to do before she put her home on the market. "Get all your home repairs done and make sure your home is pristine and in move-in condition," she said. "I don't think it's a deal breaker if your kitchen and bathrooms aren't perfect, but your home needs to be clean and clutter-free."

After Hill accepted the buyer's offer, she enlisted the services of a lawyer to handle all the legal paperwork. "When our buyer called us later that day of our open house and told us they were interested in buying, we told them our lawyer would contact their lawyer," she said. "We exchanged our lawyer's phone numbers and it was as simple as that. We let the professionals handle the legal stuff."

Although Hill did not want to enlist the services of a Realtor, she was solicited by a few agents and agreed to offer an incentive to any agent who brought in a buyer, as many FSBO sellers do. "I had a few Realtors call me once they saw the open house ad and the FSBO. They offered 2 percent commission if they brought in the owner and I agreed to it. As it turned out, we sold our own home and didn't have to give up any commission fee," she said.

Hill said she believes she was successful in selling her home on her own because she took the time to take care of all the details before she put her home on the market — she was thoroughly prepared. Her best advice for FSBO sellers includes:

- Research all local and big-city papers so you know which papers you will be listed in and put a picture of your home in the ads.

- Get all state and district scores from elementary, middle, and high schools. Each state has a different standardized test to score and rank schools. Families want to buy in areas based on schools and their scores. This is a huge selling feature.

- Know information about your town hall, parks/recreation, activities, sports, clubs, camps, and beaches. This is also a huge selling feature. Your potential buyers want to know what your town offers.

- Invite a mortgage broker who can spend the day at your home during your open house to answer questions for potential buyers.

> You will not owe the broker anything, and they will be happy to have access to potential mortgage clients.
>
> - Get quotes for home sale price from three different Realtors and then you can ballpark your selling price.
>
> - If you have a second floor, it might be a good idea to have some-one upstairs during the open house to keep watch and also to answer any questions.
>
> - Make sure your home smells good before people arrive for your open house. Have fresh-baked cookies or a pie prepared.
>
> - Have a sign-in book for everyone who walks into your home to write their name, address, phone number, and e-mail address for a follow-up.
>
> - Do not hide any problems or potential problems — get them fixed
>
> Because Hill had such a positive experience the first time around, she looks forward to selling FSBO again in the future. "I would absolutely do FSBO again and, based on my sales record, would not do anything differently. No one is going to work harder to sell your house than you. Based on friends who have had their homes on the market recently, and whose houses have sat for a long while, I would say I worked 100 percent harder than any of their realtors." Hill encourages others to list their home on their own as well, as long as others are willing to take the necessary steps and make the time commitments needed to experi-ence a successful sale. "It was all easy, and I highly recommend sell-ing your own home," she said. Visit Hill's company, Kidzsack, at **www.kidzsack.com**.

Short sales and foreclosures

While the economy has recovered from the Great Recession, some FSBO sellers might still be forced to sell their houses due to the threat of a foreclosure or a short sale. The definition of a "short sale" is a negotiation with your lender to sell the house for less than what is owed on the property. Unfortunately, this became increasingly common in the aftermath of the mortgage meltdown of 2008. While the market has broadly recovered, some sellers are still finding themselves in this position. As of early 2016, 5.1 percent of single-family home and condo sales were classified as short sales by information firm RealtyTrac.

To negotiate a short sale, begin with calling your lender and going over the details of your home ownership. If you live in a highly distressed area, are a victim of the local nature of real estate values there, or are behind on your payments, short selling is an option.

If you are only recently behind on your payments, perhaps a month or two, your lender may not be so inclined to agree to a short sale. After all, they want you to continue making your payments versus selling the house for much less than the house is worth. However, if you know that you will not be able to continue your mortgage payments, insist on the consideration of a short sale if it is the best option for you.

A short sale is often the last option for someone facing a foreclosure. A foreclosure is a legal procedure initiated by a lender to repossess a house. Despite the fact that many areas of the country are beginning to see economic improvement and growth, foreclosure rates continue to increase. Houses are typically not foreclosed until a borrower has defaulted on the mortgage for six months or longer, so borrowers who defaulted on their mortgages a year ago are just going into foreclosure now.

Realty Trac's website, **www.realtytrac.com**, is a great place to visit to get statistics on the number of foreclosures, foreclosure activity per month, and real estate trends for your area.

According to this website, the top five states with the highest foreclosure rates in the country for May 2016 are:

- New Jersey — 1 in every 558
- Maryland — 1 in every 690
- Delaware — 1 in every 711
- Florida — 1 in every 734
- Nevada — 1 in every 845

According to Foreclosure Listings Corporation (**www.foreclosure listings.com**), the top five cities with the highest foreclosure rates are:

- Miami, Florida
- Jacksonville, Florida
- Orlando, Florida
- Chicago, Illinois
- Las Vegas, Nevada

While foreclosure rates soared following the mortgage melt-down, they have abated as the market has recovered nation-wide. As of May 2016, the percentage of single-family homes that fell into default, were repossessed by a lender or were auctioned down 21 percent from May 2015, according to data from RealtyTrac. That marked the eighth consecutive month of year-over-year declines. All that said, in areas that remain economically challenged, foreclosures are still common. Foreclosure activity was especially strong in New Jersey, Maryland, Delaware, Florida, and Nevada.

Visit **www.foreclosurelistings.com** for information on foreclosures as well as foreclosure listing by state. Bank Rate, **www.bankrate. com** is also an excellent source for information on foreclosures and other market information.

So what do these numbers mean for you? If you are selling your house FSBO as a short sale, or you are selling or thinking of selling a house in an area that has a high rate of foreclosures and short sales, you must not be blind to market conditions. In either situation, it is crucial to understand what the numbers are in your area, know the challenges and how to overcome them, and know your area's real estate situation.

According to Wardell, despite the rise in foreclosures across the country, there are fewer foreclosure houses on the market. "Foreclosure filings are up, but there is no increase in the number of properties on the market," Wardell said. He speculates this is because banks are holding on to foreclosure properties to attempt to regain their value instead of selling them right away. "A $300,000 house that sells for $200,000 in a foreclosure sale is a $100,000 loss; it is not a $200,000 gain for the bank," he said. "Banks are trying to feed the foreclosure properties out at a moderate rate to increase demand and to balance the supply and demand." Banks are also hesitant to lose any more money than they have to and would rather hold onto the properties to maintain their assets until the market improves.

Selling a house in an area where there is a high rate of foreclosures and short sales can be challenging, even if your house is not a short sale or a foreclosure. People buy and sell houses because they are getting new jobs, relocating, trying to change school districts, or looking to upgrade. The areas where the rates of short sales and foreclosures are very high tend to be areas that are not the most desirable, or areas that are second-home markets, although this is not true for every market. The good neighborhoods that were well built in good locations probably did not attract a great number of subprime buyers in the first place because people were not moving out of the areas to begin with.

Foreclosures also tend to attract investors looking for a good deal versus buyers who are looking for a home to live in. This can affect your sale because some buyers do not like areas where investors instead of families own many homes, which means a high number of renters and a high turnover in the local population. People tend to want well-established, reputable neighborhoods, particularly if they have children.

Selling in a Buyer's Market

Of course, selling in a seller's market is significantly easier than selling in a buyer's market. However, people who have no choice but to sell in a buyer's market should not despair. A successful sale is still possible, but it might require a bit more patience and a little extra strategizing.

Here are some tips to selling your home in a buyer's market:

- **List your home just under market value.** You may have to price your home lower than you would like, but doing so may attract the buyer you need. It does not mean you have to price your home so low you will lose money from the sale, but pricing your home a couple of percentage points lower than similar homes in your area could attract more buyers. Visit open houses in your area and know what other similar homes in your area are selling for.

- **Check your equity.** Equity is the amount of value you have available in your home. It is determined by subtracting what you owe on the house from what is it worth. If your house is worth $150,000 and you owe $140,000, you have $10,000 worth of equity in your house. It always helps to have plenty of equity in your house; the more equity you have the less you owe to your mortgage company. If you have a lot of equity, you will be able to pocket more of the profit from the sale of your home.

- **Throw in extras.** Offer to pay half of closing costs, or include the new refrigerator and washer/dryer unit you would have otherwise not included.

- **Fix things up.** Making minimal improvements to your house can make a big difference. Curb appeal is one of the most important aspects of a home when it comes to selling, so make sure you plant some flowers, clean up your yard, clean, de-clutter, paint, and stage your home for optimal appeal.

- **Be realistic.** You may not be able to list your home for what you think it is worth or sell it as quickly as you may want to. Know your market and get in front of it.

Chapter 2

Do Your Research and Know Your Market

Every real estate market in the country has been affected differently by the overall fluctuation of the real estate market, both recently and in the past decade. What is going on in Texas may be very different from what is going on in the real estate market in Montana. The market can even vary significantly between counties, towns, and cities within a state.

Knowing your local market is important, because if you decide to sell your house, you will likely get a number of buyers who know nothing about local market real estate. Some buyers have only been listening to the news. Depending on your area, the market may not be as much of a seller's market as some buyers may think.

This lack of knowledge can sometimes make buyers somewhat unrealistic in their expectations when making offers. Many buyers do not understand that simply because a house is $125,000 in one area of town does not mean it will be or should be $125,000 in a more "desirable" area of town. A two-bedroom house in one neighborhood can easily be worth more than a four-bedroom in a nearby neighborhood.

Different Types of Buyers

Knowing your market involves knowing the variety of buyers who are looking for homes as well. Typically, homebuyers can be categorized into one of three general categories: the first-time homebuyer, a buyer purchasing his first home; the "move-up" buyer, a buyer looking to upgrade from one home to another; and the investor, a buyer looking to purchase purely as an investment.

According to Wardell, the move-up buyer barely exists in the 2009 housing market. People cannot afford to upgrade their houses or their lives nowadays, so the pool of buyers looking to upgrade their house, school system, and neighborhood has shrunk significantly. The first-time homebuyer is now much more prevalent, thanks to President Obama's tax incentives for first-time homebuyers and the amount of houses on the market under $150,000.

Naturally, the homebuyers who are ready, able, and eager to purchase are the ideal buyers. They typically know what they are looking for, and need a house fairly quickly because they have moved from out of state or have sold their previous house. The serious buyers who may not be fully ready to purchase are a bit more challenging to work with because they are usually hesitant and on the hunt for an ideal home at an ideal price and are willing to keep looking until they find it.

Investors can be challenging to work with as well because they are looking for the best deal and will sometimes attempt to convince you to sell or push you into a deal you are not comfortable with. The casual buyer who is not serious about buying and may come to your open house just to see what your house looks like and what is on the market can be very frustrating to deal with.

You will not be able to tell right away what kind of buyers are at your open houses or private showings. Often, buyers will come to an open house and show interest, talk up your home, comment on how much they like it, and then you never hear from them again. It can be an emotional roller coaster, but asking a few questions, such as the ones listed below, can help you get an idea of a buyer's intentions.

When do you plan to buy a home?

Knowing what timeframe buyers are working within can give you a good idea of how serious they are about purchasing. If they are unsure of a timeframe, the buyers are probably less of the "ready, willing, and able buyer" and more of the serious buyer shopping around, or the casual looker.

Are you pre-qualified or pre-approved for a loan?

Pre-approval means a buyer has already sat down with a lender and the lender has reviewed the buyer's finances and approved the buyer for a loan of a certain amount. A lender will typically provide a pre-approval letter to the buyer to prove pre-approval. Pre-qualification simply means a lender has determined a buyer is qualified for a loan, but has not reviewed the buyer's financials to determine how much. Pre-approval is the step beyond pre-qualification.

Do you live in the area?

The answer to this question can help you determine if the buyer is a move-up buyer or a first-time buyer and how familiar he is with the neighborhood. Certain neighborhoods — established, safe, family friendly neighborhoods with good school systems — will sell themselves. If a buyer is interested in your home for the neighborhood, you will have an easier time selling than the same house in an unattractive neighborhood.

Is this your first home purchase?

Whether or not a buyer has to sell his current home in order to buy yours is significant because it will determine how quickly you can close. If a buyer cannot close on the purchase until he closes on the sale of his current home, it will delay the process.

What are you looking for in a house?

This is a good question to ask to get a feel for what people like about your house and what they may not. You may not want to hear what people do not like, but it can really help you stay realistic about your expectations and it can help you market to the right buyer.

Are you working with a real estate agent?

This is a very important question, because it will enable you to project your closing costs, and whether you will be obligated to pay a commission to the buyer's agent. If you are 100 percent opposed to paying a buyer's agent's fee, include this in your ad so as not to waste anyone's time. Knowing whether a buyer is working with an agent from the beginning will also prevent an agent from attempting to get a commission on the sale later in the process.

Realtors are licensed real estate agents that are members of the National Association of Realtors (NAR). Only members can be designated with the Realtor logo, and not every real estate agent is a member of NAR. Agents who are not members are referred to as just "real estate agents."

Do not ask any personal questions or questions about finances, education, or job situation. The idea is to get a feel for what the buyer is looking for through general questions asked in a friendly and non-intimidating manner. If a buyer seems hesitant to answer, do not push the envelope — it is best to stop asking.

Factors That Affect a Real Estate Market

Being knowledgeable about your home's qualities in your particular area will enable you to discuss these factors with potential buyers and promote any that apply to your house.

- School systems
- Proximity to transportation
- Ideality of location
- Safety
- Condition of bathrooms and kitchen
- The overall condition of the house
- Proximity to amenities
- Access to employment in the area

School systems

School systems are one of the biggest factors for many buyers. Many families with school-age children move to certain areas because of the school systems alone, so if you live in an area with great schools, you are in better shape than someone selling in an area with a poor school system. Marketing a house for sale in a poor school district is more difficult, but it is not impossible. It may just mean you need to concentrate on more positive aspects of your house and neighborhood. You are not likely to draw in very many families with children to look at your house unless it is phenomenally priced, or perhaps the family sends their children to private school or home school. Taking out all of those families as potential buyers leaves you with a much smaller pool of prospects to pull from, and you will need to work on highlighting what is positive about your house.

Proximity to transportation

How close your house is to trains, buses, or any other mode of public transportation is a significant factor for buyers, particularly if you live on the outskirts of a major city. Garden City, for instance, is about 18 miles east of New York City and the vast majority of residents commute by train to the city for work. Houses that are in walking distance of a train station are more attractive for buyers in this area because of convenience and may even sell for a slightly higher price than a similar home on the other side of town that is not in walking distance of the train.

Ideality of location

Real estate is all about location. If your house is located in a highly demanded area, like in an established, popular neighborhood with great school systems, or in a major city, this is an important benefit for you. Houses in these areas tend to sell quickly, and for closer to listing price than others, simply because of their location.

Go to Census Reporter at **http://censusreporter.org** to search for statistics on a variety of information about population, median household income, and more for your specific city or town.

Safety

Another factor that affects a local real estate market is the crime rate. A high crime area is likely not going to yield you a premium price, as these areas tend to be less desirable. Just like marketing a house in an area with a bad school system, you will need to emphasize the positive aspects of your house instead of focusing on the crime rate. If you live in an area with low crime then you are going to be in a more desirable area and your local market is going to be better than one with higher crime rate.

Research your town or city's crime rate and get statistics at Neighborhood Scout's website at **www.neighborhoodscout. com**. The website compiles crime reports from local governments around the country and from the FBI, and enables you to search for public school information, crime rates, home appreciation rates, and general information about the area. You can also search **www.bestplaces.net** and **www.crimereports.com** for the same information.

Conditions of the bathroom and kitchen

The bathrooms and the kitchen are the most important features of a home when it comes to selling. These rooms are the most expensive and time consuming to re-model or upgrade; other rooms like bedrooms can be easily upgraded with new carpeting, a fresh coat of paint, or new light fixtures, whereas a bathroom or kitchen takes significantly more time and money to fix. If your bathrooms or kitchen are outdated, consider undertaking minimal improvements.

Overall condition of the house

Older homes tend to pose more problems than newer ones simply because older electrical, plumbing, and heating systems are more likely to need repair in the near future. If you have maintained your home well and repaired and replaced things along the way, your home will be in better condition than the one down the block that needs a new roof and a new hot water heater. Many buyers do not want a house in poor condition that will require significant repairs. However, if you are realistic about the condition of your house and price it accordingly, you may be at an advantage since there *are* a significant amount of buyers looking for "fixer-uppers," or houses that need work.

Proximity to amenities

If your house is close to restaurants, shopping, nightlife, parks, medical care, or cultural attractions you will want to use this factor to market your house. If you live in a rural area where buyers would not expect a close proximity to amenities, or in an area like a major city where buyers would *automatically* expect this, this factor will not be as significant. However, in most cases the closer you are to these amenities the better.

Access to employment in the area

This plays off the access to transportation factor. If your house is located in a major metropolitan city or suburb on the outskirts of the city with transportation, this will not be as much of a factor as a seller located in a rural farm town. If your house is in an area with factories, army bases, or some other large company that employs many people, your house will be attractive to existing employees that may want an upgraded house, or new employees who need to move to the area.

Targeting the Right Buyer

If you are in an area that has many negatives, such as high crime or poor schools, you will have to look for all the positives and highlight them. In the Oklahoma City area, there is a small community near downtown called the Paseo Arts District. It is higher in crime than other areas, the schools are not known to be very good, it looks a bit run-down and dilapidated in parts, and some would say it is not really safe after dark. If you live in an area like this, you will likely not draw in families or big spenders, so you have to be realistic. What the area does offer is the most colorful expression of architecture around town, fine art galleries, trendy eating spots, yoga, and a host of other shops with unique flair. Its popularity as a local tourist area is quickly growing and now nicer restaurants are moving in, along with a few clothing shops.

An area like this requires targeting the right buyer, and you will have to know your local area and what it has to offer in order to know what type of buyer you should be targeting. With the Paseo Arts district, for example, you will probably target a younger, trendy art lover who appreciates revitalization. You would tailor your marketing to suit, highlighting all the positives.

Prices in areas like this are generally lower, but understanding your local market, the ebbs and tides of real estate, and how to capitalize on the attractions you do have will help you sell much quicker. For instance, if you live in a wealthy, historic part of town where the schools are not great, you would not bother to point out anything about your school district but rather the positives of your neighborhood and what alternative forms of education are available. Houses like these with unique characteristics in unique communities tend to go for more in price per square foot simply due to the short supply, despite the fact that the schools system may be poor.

If you have more than a few of these factors in your favor, your house will most likely sell for more than a house with similar characteristics in an area with only one or two of these positive qualities. This helps explain why a house in Hempstead, New York, sells for far less than a similar house one town over in Garden City: schools, crime rate, and quality of homes are far different between the two although they are located within a few miles of each other.

This fact also plays into the laws of supply and demand mentioned earlier: In a more desirable community, one that boasts good schools, low crime rates, and newer houses, the demand for them is naturally higher, making the supply lower. If you own a house in one of these communities, this gives you more room to price your house a little higher.

Perception

Perception also certainly plays a part in selling your home. If the area you live in is perceived to be a high-crime area when in reality the crime statistics show otherwise, you are not likely to get a higher price per square foot as you may in another neighborhood with a more positive perception. Creating a Comparable Market Analysis (CMA) will help determine where your house stands within your neighborhood's market. A CMA is a report of all the houses in your area that are comparable to yours in terms of size, layout, and what they have sold for. The comparable properties that sold make up the worth of the houses around yours and that determines your sellable value, also known as your asking price.

Two neighborhoods that have the same quality construction of houses, similar characteristics, and a similar community can have drastically different prices when there exists just one major difference between the two, like the school systems. If one neighborhood is next to a landfill and the other one is next to a nice lake, obviously the values of the neighborhood by the lake will be higher, even if the neighborhoods are within a few miles of each other.

Regardless of where your home is located, you will most likely need to price your house competitively and do everything you can to get it in tip-top shape. Even in a buyer's market if your product is the best for the price, it will attract the most buyers and will sell quickly; people are drawn to quality.

Another aspect that can impact your local market is whether there has been a great deal of new construction in your neighborhood. With the upturn in real estate values overall in the wake of the 2008 real estate crash, new construction homes have regained their values. That said, there are always pockets of weakness, in which even relatively new homes end up in foreclosure. This can result in very good deals, which means competition for you. On the flip side, not many people can buy a house at a real estate auction with cash or with a large cash deposit, as is usually required at foreclosure sales. As a result, many people who purchase foreclosure properties are investors looking for a good deal and not families or individuals looking for a place to call home. Investors are often looking for properties like this to rent and turn a profit.

The problem with this: A neighborhood with many rentals is less attractive to a potential homebuyer and it will therefore affect your ability to sell. A family looking to buy a house and settle down does not want to live where the neighbors are constantly changing and the properties are not cared for in the way an owner would care for property. It also makes the neighborhood transient and presents the chance for it to change quickly from a good neighborhood to a less-favorable one.

You should consider selling to an investor if you are selling in an area with a high rental or foreclosure rate, and if you are eager to quickly sell. You may not get as much for the house, but you also will likely not have to make repairs and do as much marketing. You will save money getting it sold because you will not have to continue making house payments, provided you have a mortgage.

Real estate values can vastly differ from one neighborhood to another. The variation may not be great, but if you live in an area that is considered "sought-after," you can get a higher price per square foot based on that alone than if you live in one five minutes away that is no longer sought-after. Selling in the less-marketable neighborhoods has its advantages as well; the more popular neighborhoods are often newer, with stricter requirements made by the developer and enforced by the homeowners association. This can actually turn people away — owners do not want to be told they cannot install a pool or put up a storage shed. Older, more established neighborhoods usually offer this kind of flexibility, which is marketable. You can point this out on your fliers and in your online marketing if it is applicable. On the other hand, some well established communities, like the previously mentioned Garden City, New York, have strict rules and zoning regulations that have been in place for many years that are difficult to challenge.

Chapter 3

Determine If FSBO is For You and Know What to Avoid

FSBO is not for everyone. It is crucial to understand all of the factors and requirements that come along with selling on your own before you embark on doing so. The process will take a considerable amount of time, patience, energy, research, and perhaps money. Being prepared for all these will make your experience much more rewarding.

The FSBO Facts

There are a myriad of "facts" out there about FSBO sales and statistics, but it is unfortunately difficult to grasp an accurate understanding in numbers of how many homes are sold FSBO per year on a national level. The National Association of Realtors (NAR) is a national organization with more than 1 million Realtors members nationwide. According to data from NAR, the number of

FSBOs has declined in recent years. The group says that in 2015, FSBOs fell to 8 percent of all sales last year. That represents a 9 percent decline since 2012 and the least since 1981, when it began gathering such data.

But that doesn't mean people should skip this option. For those who strategize carefully, the FSBO approach offers tremendous benefits. For that reason, some FSBO proponents predict such sales are poised to soar over the next few years.

There are several websites and blogs, such as the best-known For Sale by Owner website **www.forsalebyowner.com** and the For Sale by Owner Blog, **http://blog.forsalebyowner.com**, that challenge the accuracy of the NAR statistics and this claim. Some FSBO websites claim these stats do not take into account FSBO sellers who use some help, such as discount brokerages or MLS services. Some of these websites claim FSBO sales are much higher per year, closer to 20 percent of all home sales, and that FSBOs are actually on the rise.

The facts vary depending on where you look and whom you ask. Regardless of this, however, FSBO sales account for a significant amount of home sales per year, which is a positive sign that FSBOs have a strong presence in the marketplace.

The FSBO checklist

Whether you have decided to sell FSBO already or are still weighing your options, the following questions will give you an idea of how ready you are to sell on your own. If you are hesitant on any answers, you may need to do more research before you put your home on the market.

1. **Are you willing to dedicate an indefinite amount of time to this process?** You cannot put a time frame on

selling, although you should try your best to get it sold within the first 30 days it is on the market.

2. **Are you prepared to adjust to any hold-ups in the process?** Hold-ups could result from anything including an inspection, appraisal, or the negotiation- and contract-signing process. Be sure you are willing and able to take the time that may be necessary should the process hit a speed bump.

3. **Are you willing to price accurately and be realistic about expectations?** Understanding your market and pricing accurately will determine whether or not you house sells. If you are not realistic about your expectations, the process could prove very challenging.

4. **Are you willing to host open houses each month and show strangers your house?** Open houses and showings are your ticket to exposing your house to the public and attracting a buyer. Make sure you are prepared to commit the time and energy it will take to show people your home and answer questions.

5. **Are you willing to clean, de-clutter, and make any necessary repairs and improvements to your home?** This process involves identifying problems in your house and then strategizing ways to fix these problems, which is often hard to do. Soliciting neighbors and friends for an honest opinion can help, so be prepared to do this.

6. **Are you ready to listen to faults or negative aspects about your house that buyers may point out?** This is often hard to do also, but you will ultimately come across it and knowing your house's negative attributes will help keep your expectations in check when it comes to pricing.

7. **Are you ready to ask buyers questions that may be awkward or uncomfortable, such as questions about their ability to obtain a loan?** One of the things FSBO sellers do not like about the process is handling communication like this with buyers. It can certainly be uncomfortable, but asking the right questions and ensuring your buyers are qualified and able to purchase your house will only save you time and money in the long run.

8. **Are you comfortable negotiating?** This is another aspect of the process that many FSBO sellers are not comfortable with. You need to be able to treat selling your house as a business transaction and remove yourself from any personal involvement, which will make negotiating much easier.

9. **Are you comfortable handling the legal paperwork involved in the process?** Many FSBO sellers enlist an attorney to handle the legal paperwork, which is the best option unless you are confident you are 100 percent familiar with not only all the legal requirements involved, but how to draft a contract that is in your best interest that protects you as the seller.

10. **Are you confident you can create and manage a marketing plan?** Being familiar with the Internet is nearly a necessity for creating an effective marketing plan. You should be familiar with your local papers and be prepared to place an advertisement in these, along with other places around your neighborhood and beyond.

11. **Are you informed about all of the aspects of the process, from listing to closing?** Besides the paperwork and closing process, selling a home is a fairly simple process as long as you are familiar with the steps. Make sure you are comfortable with each step before you put your house on the market.

12. **Do you have a Plan B?** Things do not always go as planned, and selling a house is no exception. There are a variety of things that can go wrong, from an unexpected problem found during inspection to a buyer who cannot get a mortgage after two weeks of negotiating. Be prepared for anything, and always have a Plan B in case something unexpected goes wrong.

What to Avoid

When you sell your house on your own without the guidance of a Realtor, it becomes no one else's responsibility but yours to understand the process and all the aspects of a selling a home. While you can certainly enlist people to help you with targeted areas along the way, such as a real estate attorney, marketing expert, or designer, you alone have the responsibility to understand these details.

Knowing what *not* to do can be just as valuable as knowing what *to* do when it comes to selling your home on your own. As with anything, being knowledgeable about the entire process and all its requirements before you commit to initiating that process is always the best way to approach a task. While selling your home on your own can be a straightforward, easy, and very manageable process, there are a number of things you should avoid in order to make the most out of your FSBO experience. These tips on what to avoid can help you maintain control over the process and optimize your success in selling your home.

Pricing too high and expecting too much

One of the biggest mistakes FSBO sellers make is pricing too high. This is often because FSBO sellers do not know what their homes are worth and do not take the time to do a comparative market analysis and accurately price their homes. Although you may have your own thoughts on how much your home should sell for, it is ultimately buyers and the status of the market that determine the value of a home. It is imperative to research your local market and know where your home stands in comparison. You will then be able to price your home effectively and draw more potential buyers.

On the other hand, some people do put their homes up for sale at a higher price just to see if it gets any bids; after all, you just need one buyer to fall in love with the property and be willing to pay what you are asking. If you do list your home above market value, be prepared to either reduce your price or sit on the home for a while. The problem with pricing higher is you miss the initial opportunity to get the house sold quickly, and you take the risk of letting it sit on the market for more than 30 days, the golden period. Once buyers see the home has been on the market for a few months, your home may become less attractive. You can avoid putting yourself in this position by pricing your home correctly when you first put it on the market.

Believing everything you hear

Sometimes, sellers are so eager to sell their houses they lose their sense of reason at times and forget to take the necessary steps to protect themselves. This happens often when buyers fall in love with your house. Take this scenario for example: A potential buyer comes to look at your home, tells you he loves it and want to a bid in on it, and is ready to write a contract and make an earnest money deposit. You take the buyer's word that he is serious about his commitment to buy without asking to see a letter of pre-qualification from a mortgage company. Because you think you have a serious bid, you cancel your open house for the following week, stop taking calls, stop showing the house, and maybe even take the house off the market. A few weeks later, you find out the buyers have terrible credit and were never approved for a mortgage. Now you have lost selling days and the chance to get exposure with an open house; you have also lost the energy you put into the resources to prepare for the open house that you cancelled because you thought the house was sold.

To avoid a situation like this, ask for proof of qualification from a certified lender to purchase a home. You are your only advocate and a serious, qualified buyer will completely understand that you need this information and will not be offended that you are asking for it.

Not checking qualifications

Even if a buyer comes to you with a letter stating she is pre-qualified for a mortgage, you should always want to speak with the buyer's lender to verify the lender is reputable. Lenders generally fall into three categories: banks and credit unions, mortgage brokers, and mortgage bankers. Furthermore, there are two types of financing qualifications a buyer can have: a pre-qualification and a pre-approval.

Banks and credit unions

It may seem that if someone is qualified through a banking institution it must be a legitimate loan, but this is not always the case. In fact, many banks are slow at getting loans closed on time because banks do not specialize in making loans exclusively like mortgage bankers and brokers. Because of this, they generally do not get the best mortgage loan originators since they simply do not handle the volume of loans that are done by institutions that focus exclusively on real estate lending. A good loan originator knows the ins and outs of the entire process and the requirements of each individual underwriting lender. They also know how to spot a problem before it escalates into a deal breaker, which is one of the benefits to having a loan with a mortgage banker or broker over a traditional bank.

Additionally, many banks use outside underwriting lenders, the same ones every other lender uses. So the loan is not actually coming directly from that bank and therefore not completely in their control. Commercial banks like Citibank, Bank of America, and Chase are not primarily mortgage lenders. Mortgage lending is the primary business of savings and loans associations, some smaller banks, and financial institutions.

Despite these issues, however, loans from banks are not always troublesome; just do your homework to ensure the bank has the means and experience to support the buyer's loan. Here are some questions to ask a buyer about the bank that is offering them the loan:

- **How much experience does the loan originator have?** If the loan originator has been there for three months and the bank started making loans a year ago, you might prepare for a delay.

- **How long has the bank been making loans?** It will be riskier to take a loan with a company that is not experienced with originating loans. Taking a loan with a commercial bank like Citibank, even though their primary business is not making loans, is not necessarily a bad idea. Check what kind of rates you can get first and then compare.

- **Is the loan being made by the bank itself or an outside lender?** If a bank or financial institution is planning to sell your loan to the secondary loan market, then it may muddle things because your lender will change. While it is common practice for loans to be sold to a different company, it can be risky particularly in a challenging economic time like 2007 to 2009 and possibly beyond. With companies going out of business and filing for bankruptcy, it is best to try to stick with the original lender.

- **What is the average length of time from contract to closing?** The shorter the amount of time, the better for you because the quicker you can close and get your money. Usually, closing takes place 45-60 days after a contract signing but can be much longer.

Mortgage brokers

By definition, a mortgage broker acts as an intermediary who sells mortgage loans on behalf of individuals or businesses. In other words, mortgage brokers do not actually make the loan themselves. A mortgage broker is a go-between from the buyer to the underwriting lender. Good mortgage brokers will be honest with a lender about their options, such as the best type of loan for the client, and will not push a buyer into committing to a loan they cannot afford. Fortunately, the likelihood of brokers lending to buyers who cannot afford the loan are much lower thanks to the market crash of 2008. Unfortunately, there may still be some mortgage brokers who are willing to cross ethical and even legal lines to get a loan closed.

One way to determine if you are dealing with a reputable broker is to look him or her up through the Better Business Bureau (**www.bbb.org**). Once you get to the website, enter your local ZIP code, and you will automatically be directed to the local chapter of the Better Business Bureau. Click on "Check Out a Business or Charity" and enter the name of the broker's company. You will be able to see detailed information about the company's standing, reviews, and a grade for the business.

Keep in mind that if the broker company has not subscribed to the BBB, the company cannot be notified. Therefore, even if one person complains, the company receives a low rating. The BBB has to note the complaint as "un-responded" even though the company is unaware of the complaint. If the company you look up has a bad rating, research the reason because the company could have simply never subscribed to the BBB.

You can also contact a local title company and ask them of their experience working with a particular lender and what the experience was like when closing with the lender. Recommendations are the best way to confirm the validity and capability of a company or professional.

You should check out the lender *before* you sign any contract. Depending on what you find, you may want to write a contingency in the contract to protect yourself that states the sale is contingent upon full loan approval and you as the seller will continue to show your home and take back-up offers until the loan approval is confirmed and in writing.

Sample Phone Script

"Hi, this Sue Johnson and I am selling my house for sale by owner. I have an offer from a buyer who is using ABC Lending; have you heard of them? If so, what was your experience in dealing with them? If not, can you direct me as to who can tell me if they are a reputable lender? Is there anything else you think I should know to protect myself and the buyer?" Feel free to ask the title company if they know how long the bank has been offering loans and if it is a reputable bank in the industry.

Mortgage bankers

Mortgage bankers are the best type of lender because they specialize in making mortgage loans and actually underwrite and service those loans. Because they specialize in making mortgage loans and nothing else, they have the knowledge, experience, and quality of product to help ensure a smooth process. Because they are the ones actually making the loan, they are careful to ensure a buyer is qualified. After all, it is their own investment and if they are not careful to qualify the buyers properly and get things done in a timely manner, they will miss the deal as well.

Mortgage bankers usually have a well-qualified staff that handles all the details of the loan process. They also have advanced experience in dealing with unique and challenging issues that arise in a real estate transaction, since making real estate loans is all they do, as opposed to a bank that dabbles in many ventures. If your buyer is working with a mortgage banker, certainly make contact with the loan officer and get proof of the qualification.

Correspondent lenders

Almost all mortgages currently sold on the secondary market are being sold to the big banks either from each other or from correspondent lenders. A correspondent lender is someone who specializes in originating mortgages with the company's own money and underwriters, but then sells the loan on the secondary market. These lenders are actually much faster and more efficient at closing your mortgage, because that is all they do. They do not service loans and do not deal with bank deposits. Correspondent lenders typically close loans in 30 days, so they save a considerable amount of time.

Whomever your buyer is working with, your goal is to obtain the preapproval letter and not just a prequalification letter. A prequalification letter simply states that based on the information the buyer verbally gave the lender, the buyer could qualify for a loan. A preapproval letter, on the other hand, states that the mortgage loan officer has actually verified that information and, based on that, the buyer is approved for the loan.

For example, say a buyer tells a loan company over the phone that she has a monthly income of $3,500 before taxes. Based on that information, the lender would probably issue a prequalification letter to the buyer for a specified amount based on that income. A buyer cannot get preapproved until she actually shows the lender her paystubs. When you contact the lender, make sure the lender has certified the information is correct and the buyer is preapproved rather than just prequalified.

Getting too emotional

Selling a house is an emotional experience. If you are selling your house on your own without the help of a Realtor, you will need to detach yourself from the emotional ties you may have to your house and look at the process as a business transaction. This is particularly important when you are hosting potential buyers in an open house or showing. You may love the color of your living room, but a buyer may not and may feel free to comment how much he dislikes it. Similarly, you think you have beautiful landscaping in your backyard, but a potential buyer could comment on how he would rip it out to install a pool.

Beyond that, if you do not step back and learn to relax, you will be anxious throughout the process and it will only prove to be more difficult than it needs to be. Things will likely come up during the process, and the house is not closed until the check is in the bank, so staying calm and collected in the meantime will help ensure a smooth process for everyone.

Cutting corners

Selling your home on your own is undoubtedly a process that requires a significant amount of work. Simply putting a sign in the yard will not necessarily cut it, even in a seller's market.

When it comes to marketing and advertising, it is essential to choose the right avenues for advertising your home. Some websites are a waste of money and will not help you get your house sold. MLS and other websites will be discussed in detail in Chapter 6. When it comes to advertising your FSBO, cutting corners will simply not do you any good. Similarly, cutting corners when it comes to cleaning and staging your home and handling important aspects of the process like the legal paperwork will also likely yield consequences. If you cut corners on paperwork, for instance, and decide to save money and not hire a real estate attorney or similar professional to draw up your contract and oversee the closing process, you may face delays in closing if the paperwork is incorrect.

Deals that sound too good to be true

There are buyers out there who "prey" on FSBOs and attempt to purchase your house for the lowest possible price. According to Christa Michael — a real estate agent in the Atlanta, Georgia area — some investors will attempt to take advantage of FSBO sellers. A common scheme among these investors is to convince the seller to sell the investor the home but keep the mortgage in the seller's name. Michael has seen this happen to some FSBO sellers, and many sign contracts and do not even realize the investor has included such a clause. The result can be devastating, and can prevent the seller from being able to mortgage a new home. Make sure you feel comfortable with a buyer and understand every clause of a contract before signing anything.

Getting in over your head

Many FSBO sellers think it will be easy to sell on their own, and they realize down the road that selling FSBO is not for them. It is perfectly fine to realize you want to hire a Realtor — if you do so before you get too far along in the process. According to Michael, a real estate agent legally cannot get involved in a deal to represent you after you have signed a contract. This is why understanding what you are signing is so important: you may legally bind yourself to a deal you later decide is not right for you. More often than not, the deal is too far along to back out after a contract has been signed.

Turning off potential buyers

If you are anxious to get your home on the market and rush the cleaning and staging processes, for instance, you may turn off potential buyers. The condition of your home makes a significant impression on the buyer. If a buyer walks into your home and it is in disarray, the buyer may assume you are also incapable of caring for your home and, therefore, the house may have some problems. A first impression is the most important, and you have just once chance to make a good one.

Even in markets with many homes available, many buyers are going to be picky. This is a huge investment for them, and you can expect that they will ask many questions and that you will have to spend a significant amount of time responding to these questions and working out details. If you are not open, friendly, and knowledgeable about your home and your neighborhood, you can expect buyers to be hesitant about purchasing your home.

Being unaware of your market

This goes back to pricing correctly. If you do not know your local market and what homes in the area are selling for, you will not be able to price competitively to sell. Knowing details about your school system, transportation options, taxes, community and outreach centers, zoning laws, and general neighborhood statistics will help you attract the right buyer.

The Pros and Cons of FSBO

Like with anything, selling a house FSBO has its advantages and disadvantages. Selling a house is one of the biggest financial transactions most people ever make, and it can be very taxing on your emotions as well. Whether you have already made up your mind to sell by owner and you are considering it, but need more facts and information, knowing the pros and cons will help you to be more prepared for the process, helping to alleviate the kind of surprises that might discourage you had you not known what to expect.

The pros

You will save money

Realtors charge an average of six percent of the sale price of a house for their services, split between the seller's agent and the buyer's agent, if there is one. Even in a strong market like the one the U.S. is currently experiencing, it makes sense for sellers to cut costs at every turn. Saving money by selling your house yourself results in some of the biggest savings you can see in a financial transaction. Take a look at the chart below to get an idea of how much selling FSBO could save you.

Sales Price	6 percent charged by Realtor
$150,000	$9,000
$250,000	$15,000
$350,000	$21,000
$500,000	$30,000
$1,000,000	$60,000

Granted, you will have to take at least a portion of the money you would save and apply it to marketing your house, any repairs, and other related expenses. However, these will not add up to nearly six percent of the cost of your house. Six percent of the sales price of your house is a significant amount of money for services you can do on your own or with minimal help. When every penny counts, selling FSBO yields you a significant savings.

You maintain control

Selling a house is not only requires time and patience, it is a significant emotional investment as well. No one cares about your house as much as you do, and many people are reluctant to hand over the control of selling it to a stranger. When you use a Realtor, you forfeit a significant level of control over your transaction. Maintaining control of every aspect of the transaction can help you get your house sold faster. It is simply not possible for a Realtor, who has dozens of other listings, to give yours the attention that you can.

Selling your house yourself eliminates the concern that something is being mishandled or neglected. The unfortunate truth is Realtors are trained to sell and make money, and it does not require a significant amount of training for someone to get a real estate license compared to other professions. There are many Realtors who are great at their job, but there are many that are not really equipped to handle one of the most important and involved transactions. In many cases, a Realtor's strength is in marketing and not necessarily the legal aspects of selling a house.

Some Realtors also do not take sufficient time to get to know all the aspects and facts about your house before they put it on the market as many are eager to get it listed and sold, and it can end up costing you a sale. When you use a Realtor, you are also subject to letting him know everything about your house and the sale, when you are out of town, when you want to change your price, have an open house, or make repairs on the house. Selling FSBO eliminates this third party and enables you to have complete control over your transaction, working on your time and at your discretion.

CASE STUDY: PRACTICING CONSULTATIVE REAL ESTATE

Erica Ramus

To Realtor Erica Ramus, selling a home means a lot more than putting a sign in a yard. "A good agent — buyer's agent or seller's agent — these days is more than just showing houses to people," Ramus said. "Buyers don't need us as much to find houses (thanks to the Internet) and sellers don't need us as much to get the word out. What they both need are our brains and our skills, to navigate them through this complicated process."

Ramus has a background in marketing and publishing — she owned her own magazine for more than a decade that she recently sold — and in 2000 decided to get her real estate license. In 2007, Ramus started her own firm, a franchise of Realty Executives: a real estate franchise company with thousands of franchises around the world.

Ramus began working with FSBOs when she first started in the business, although she did not find soliciting these types of sellers easy. "Before I started my own company, I used to solicit FSBOs and discovered many really don't want to talk to agents at all," she said. "They will avoid an agent like the plague." In her experience, sellers were very reluctant to hire agents who tried to convince them to list with them, and rightfully so.

"[The sellers] probably have dozens of people knocking on their door, sending them letters, telling them they are going to fail and when they do, to call them. One FSBO who eventually did list with me showed me the letters he received [from agents], and he was offended by their arrogant, show-off manner. The seller saved the letter and stewed over it. He was put off by the tone of the letter and said he'd never hire that guy," Ramus said.

This particular seller did end up hiring Ramus "because I didn't tell him he was stupid and couldn't get the job done. I listened to his problem and offered him a solution that benefited both of us," she said. "I run a full-service firm. I am not a cut-rate or discount broker. However, I offer a menu of services and tailor the product to each particular situation. I don't walk into an appointment and say 'This is my fee, take it or leave it,'" she said.

Ramus' first step is to approach the seller nicely, and not as an authority figure. "I first have a conversation with the sellers and find out their motivation for moving, to go over their financial situation, and assess their exact needs. Then I present my services and see how we can work together to achieve the same goals: the house gets sold, and I am compensated for my work. I consider it practicing consultative real estate. If there is no meeting of the minds, or we don't 'gel' at this meeting, there is no use moving forward. I just wish the seller good luck, leave with him or her some information they'll need to sell their home by themselves in Pennsylvania, and move on."

This approach has worked successfully for Ramus and her company from day one. "My theory is that some buyers and sellers need more or less help than others," she said. Why should there be one flat fee for everyone, no matter how much work is involved? If a client wants less or more done, they should pay accordingly," she explained.

"Most agents see FSBOs as the enemy — people who want to take food from their mouths. I see them as sellers who don't think they need representation. Some do and some don't. Some sellers think that all we do is put a sign in the yard. Some have been burned in the past and had bad experiences with Realtors. Some think this job is easy and they can do it as well as anyone else. Some are short money and don't want to or cannot pay a Realtor a commission," explained Ramus.

In her extensive experience with FSBOs over the years, Ramus has noticed a general trend: "I see most FSBOs either succeed pretty quickly in finding a buyer, or not. There doesn't seem to be much middle ground. If FSBO sellers don't find a buyer in the first month or two, their chances diminish and they get discouraged."

And when they don't succeed, they call Ramus to handle the marketing. In this situation, Ramus would charge a percentage fee. Her firm also offers MLS service, which incorporates a buyer's agent's fee. "When we're entering the data in a MLS service, we must offer a co-broke to the other broker, so we step into the percentage fee territory," she said.

What many FSBO sellers do not understand is that selling a home, regardless of whether you list with an agent or sell on your own, is a long and involved process. "Finding a buyer is just step one in a long list of things that must be done to close a deal," Ramus said. "Finding a buyer who loves your home and wants to buy it is great. Then they have to qualify for a loan, deal with home inspectors and appraisers, and make it to closing."

Today, Ramus mainly lists properties while the agents in her office work directly with buyers. While she has seen many FSBOs succeed in her years of business, many of them end up calling her back and listing their home with her firm. "Sometimes they put a sign out, and sell it quickly," she said. But some of them realize selling FSBO is not for them. "The biggest complaints I hear from FSBO sellers are: They didn't realize how frustrating it is to have so many people go through your house, say nice things, then disappear, never to call you again; they don't know how to and don't feel comfortable qualifying people over the phone before they let them come in; and they get worn down and tired of showing the home and getting no offers," Ramus said.

Ramus' best advice for those considering FSBO is to not get too involved in the emotional aspects of the transaction — it should not blur the fact that it is a business transaction. FSBO sellers need to be on their guard and not get too emotionally invested in the deal. They have to try to not make it personal. It's a business transaction and they need to step away from the deal and see it from a more distant perspective," she said. "This is hard in the heat of negotiating." In the end, she said, what FSBOs seller need most to make their sale successful is distance and perspective.

More wiggle room in the price

The biggest reason a house sits on the market for a long period of time is almost always a result of the price. If a home is not priced correctly and cannot compete with similar homes in the area (meaning the other homes are priced lower and selling faster), you are at a disadvantage. There is a selling price for everything, and you need to be able to find the price it will take to sell your house. Realtors want to take the most profit possible and they will oftentimes encourage you to list the house for a higher price than you may feel comfortable listing it for.

If you do not use a Realtor, you can price three to six percent lower than you would if you listed it with one, depending on if the buyer has an agent, who would get three percent. Of course, you want to make selling on your own worthwhile and make a profit, but if you need to sell your home quickly, being able to price your house six percent lower than similar homes in your area listed with an agent will give you a big advantage. It can mean the difference between getting the house sold and having a house that sits.

For example, if you are planning to list your house for sale at $220,000, with a Realtor you would pay a commission of six percent, or $13,200. If you list the house without a Realtor, you can now list it at $206,800 without losing any money. Assuming you are competitively priced and you sell yourself instead of paying a Realtor, you have extra negotiating room in the price.

It is, of course, important that you price right from the start. Unless you are just putting your house on the market to see if you get a bite and are not very interested in selling, good pricing and having room to move are the most important aspects.

The house may sell faster

In a buyer's market, most sellers have a goal of selling fast. There are far too many houses sitting on the market in a buyer's market to play with the price. Selling the house yourself gives you the ability to price lower than you would with a Realtor.

The most opportune time to sell a house is within the first 30 days it is on the market. After that, your newly listed house becomes old news in the community and the excitement period passes. Being able to control your own timeline allows you to optimize these first 30 days and attract the right buyer before this period ends.

This flexibility also gives you the option to assist the buyer with lender allowable closing costs if need be. Allowable closing costs are closing costs that can be charged to the buyer in addition to a down payment. These generally include but are not limited to:

- Loan fees
- Attorney fees
- Title insurance fees
- Home inspection fees
- Appraisal costs

The FHA details specific costs that are allowable, therefore payable by the buyers, and those that are not allowable and cannot be charged to the buyer. Tax service fees, for instance, are a non-allowable closing cost, meaning the buyer cannot be charged for this fee. Appraisal costs and credit report costs on the other hand, are allowable costs.

Though many of the no-money-down programs are no longer offered, there are still programs available to assist buyers with limited resources for a down payment and closing costs, like an FHA loan. Selling on your own also presents the option to offer a seller some kind of credit or assistance, either through paying for a portion of the closing costs or offering seller financing. The option to do this does still exist if you list with a Realtor, but you will have much more flexibility if you sell on your own. The ability to offer seller assistance opens your house up for more buyers who need this kind of help, which may help your house sell faster.

You learn something and grow as a person

Selling a house is an emotional experience. Everything you do in your life that pushes you out of your comfort zone and teaches you something is nothing less than positive. Even if it is difficult and sometimes challenging to complete the task, selling your home yourself is a great opportunity for you to learn and grow as a person. There is the growth in learning how to interact with people, gather information, and complete tasks; and the experience of obtaining new skills, such as how to market your home and manage important financial transactions.

It is also an opportunity for your family to pull together and accomplish something together. When the house is sold, you will feel good about yourself and what you accomplished, and you can help others do the same. Even if you are selling because you are in a difficult situation and you need to sell, perhaps you are behind on your mortgage or facing a drop in income, it is still a big accomplishment to focus on a task and get it done. You will feel good about yourself for sticking it out and making it happen.

The cons

Selling on your own is time-consuming

Selling your house yourself can be very time consuming. In addition to the time it takes to show it and take phone calls, simply keeping the house in showing condition all the time can be challenging. Your ultimate goal is to turn interested callers into scheduled showings. In order to do this, you must prepare your home and keep it clean until it sells. A clean, tidy, organized, and de-cluttered house has much more of a chance of selling than one that is messy and disorganized, so this is a very important aspect of selling your house.

Many things involved in selling a house can take valuable time out of your life. Before you list your house, you will have to invest time to prepare it for sale, which includes painting, cleaning, staging, and repairing. Of course, once those things are done you have to keep it in pristine condition all the time — you never know when you might get a call from someone ready to look as soon as you can show the house. You must dedicate the time to invest in the process and be prepared to show your home whenever a buyer is interested or you will risk losing a potential sale.

If you list with a Realtor, however, you will still be required to rearrange your schedule for interested buyers and open houses. Realtors often like when homeowners are not present at open houses and showings; it just makes it easier to limit the amount of people in the home and enables the Realtor to do his job without the interference of the homeowner. If you choose to not be present when your Realtor shows your house or hosts an open house, you will still need to commit the time to accommodate this.

You will have to develop marketing strategies

After you have prepared the house, you must prepare the strategies and materials that will actually aid you in the selling process, which include fliers, pictures, signs, and possibly a website or online presence.

Particularly if you are not technologically savvy, learning to navigate the Web can be very challenging and time consuming. If you are able to invest money to hire a marketing company or designer to create a Web page and Web presence for you, this could be a good investment that would allow you to concentrate on other marketing materials.

Making fliers and creating ads for newspapers and local publications also takes a considerate amount of time. You must have knowledge of basic design programs to make these materials look professional, as you will be competing with homes in your area for sale that may be listed with a Realtor and have professionally created marketing materials.

Developing an effective flier is somewhat of an art, and is very important to the success of your marketing. You will want to take your time and make sure it is informative enough but not filled with so much information about the house the buyer feels there is no need to even see the house. You will also need to ensure everything is spelled correctly and includes all of the crucial information to optimize your potential for attracting buyers.

Once you create your flier, they need to be replaced and updated with any new information if necessary. If you are not getting any calls, you need to be constantly looking for new ways to market and new places to expose your house. There are marketing companies and services you can hire to initiate and manage this process, which will be discussed in details in Chapter 6.

Handling all those phone calls

After the groundwork is behind you and your house is officially on the market, taking calls from potential buyers comes next. If you have a high-quality product at a great price, then chances are you receive a lot of inquiry about it. Buyers tend to call about FSBOs more than properties listed with Realtors because of the potential for a reduced price, a great deal, and simply because they tend to feel safer about the purchase because the home is listed directly by the owner.

These calls can also come from real estate agents and other professionals in the business looking for the listing and/or your business. You should be prepared to handle these calls as well, as some agents can actually help you by bringing buyers to your home (See Chapter 6 for more information on this topic).

It may become frustrating to handle all the inquiries, especially from people who may not be serious about purchasing your home but are just curious about details like pricing and square footage. You will also experience this during an open house, when neighbors and other people not in the market for a new home come simply to check it out.

To deal with the phone calls and inquiries, some home sellers decide they will let all the calls go to voicemail and weed out the people they wish to call back from there. While this may save you a great deal of time, you may miss a great opportunity. Many people will not stay interested for long, and catching the interest of a potential buyer and setting up an appointment to view the house as soon as possible may mean the difference between a sale or not. Some people are ready, willing, and able buyers who also happen to be impatient or simply have minimal time to find a home. Finding the time and the right balance for your schedule is quite challenging.

Knowing all the details of your home and surrounding community

To optimize your potential for selling you house quickly and for the highest price possible, you will have to be very familiar with your neighborhood, especially with the school statistics. Since schools are very important to buyers, knowing about them even if you do not have children or firsthand experience with the system will be extremely helpful. It is also wise to know your neighborhood's crime statistics. It can be slightly tedious to do this research and memorize some of it to rattle off to potential buyers, but very worth it. To find out information on your community, visit your town's website or go to your local library. The FedStats website, **www.fedstats.gov**, is a great resource to find various statistics like these about your county and city.

You will have to handle contracts and paperwork

One of the most important things to remember in a transaction as important and permanent as selling a home is to put every single thing in writing. If you are not comfortable with handling the paperwork and the legal aspects of selling a home, you will either have to invest the time to familiarize yourself with this, or you will have to hire someone, probably an attorney, to manage this for you. This, of course, takes time and money, but you do not want to find yourself in a legal situation with no proof of something agreed to verbally. Knowing what you are doing from the beginning will prevent this.

If you do not hire an attorney to prepare or review legal paperwork for you, it is imperative that you understand it thoroughly yourself. This paperwork includes contracts and other closing documents, tax forms, and seller's disclosure forms, among many others, some of which are included on the accompanying CD-ROM. The closing process can be very confusing if you do not understand it fully in order to act in your own best interest.

You will also have to understand how to correctly document disclosures. Filling out a set of seller's disclosures should be done before you even put the property on the market.

Most sellers are required to disclose certain types of information about the homes they are selling. This is done on a form that has many detailed questions regarding the history and condition that you must answer truthfully.

You will have to handle problems and know how to negotiate

Unless you are a detail-oriented person, tending to the little details of every aspect of selling your house can be challenging. However, missing these details can cost you a sale. If you get a buyer who is very interested in your house but is hesitant because your appliances are out of date or the backyard is not landscaped, you will have to be prepared to negotiate with the buyer. This may mean reducing your price or offering to install new appliances or fix the backyard. Some people find it difficult to negotiate with buyers, and this is one of the drawbacks of not having a real estate agent do this for you. The perfect house does not exist any more than the perfect person exists — but buyers do expect that the major areas of your house will be working properly. Some buyers are much more detailed, and expect things like new appliances or landscaping.

As a For Sale by Owner seller, you will have to be ready to deal with and fix problems that an inspector finds in his or her inspection report. Often, the inspection is the worst part of the process because it can make or break a sale. Homeowners are often unpleasantly surprised to discover problems with their homes that an inspector will find. The inspector will almost always find something wrong with your house and it is always better to have someone experienced in that particular field make the repair.

The title can also have problems, which can be a headache to deal with. "Title work" refers to documents prepared by the title company that outline the ownership of the property and other various details. Handling the title and transfer of that title is one significant reason you will want to close with an escrow company. An "escrow" is a trust account, often held by a third party such as a bank or recognized escrow company, where funds are deposited until the terms of a contract have been met. When these certain conditions have been met, the money or property is released to the seller.

There are a variety of issues that can arise that would prevent or delay the release of funds from escrow, and therefore, the sale of the house. For example, if a seller filed for bankruptcy ten years ago and the bank technically owns the home he is now trying to sell, it can void the entire sale and cause significant problems. The good news is that title and escrow problems can almost always be solved, although they will most likely cause a delay in closing. One of the best things about involving a third party in your home sale, such as a Realtor, is to manage the details between the buyer and the seller. Selling your home on your own will eliminate this third party and you will be responsible for all communication with potential buyers. It can often be difficult to communicate and negotiate until both parties are content, particularly if you are dealing with a difficult buyer.

You must be wise in handling every communication and interaction with a buyer and put everything in writing. Depending on the circumstances of the sale and condition of your house, you may even have to put *what you will not do* in writing. Lack of experience in negotiating and communicating can lead to mistakes and misunderstandings and you will have to do your best to avoid both. You can do that by including every detail of your transaction, such as any home repairs or things that will come with the sale in your contract, which will eliminate confusion and controversy. For instance, if you as a seller acknowledge that the carpets in your house are inadequate and slightly dirty, the buyer may interpret this to mean that you will be replacing the carpets. Having everything in writing and understanding how to clearly communicate will minimize misunderstandings such as these.

You will have an increased liability

Unfortunately, even if you were unaware of a problem or that something was handled wrong when *you* purchased your home, you can still be held accountable. When you choose to sell on your own, you are the sole person responsible if a problem arises. When others are involved such as a Realtor, lawyer, or licensed repair workers, then you have someone else to look to for guidance and someone to hold accountable if something goes wrong.

As you can see, there are a variety of pros and cons that come along with selling your house on your own. Many of these cons, such as keeping your home clean and de-cluttered and being ready to show your home at any time, you will face regardless of how you sell your home — whether by a FSBO or listed with a Realtor. The good news is that although almost every closing has a hitch or two, most problems can be dealt with fairly easily.

The most important thing to do is research before you list your home, and gather your resources. Knowing what you are getting into and being aware of the requirements will help to ensure your home sale is successful for all parties. Fortunately, there are many places to turn for help and information. Escrow companies and closing agencies as well as title companies are usually very knowledgeable about all aspects of home buying and selling, including your state's laws and requirements.

If you are prepared to give the process all you have and are realistic in your expectations, you will be in a great position to sell your house on your own. The next step is preparing your house for sale.

Chapter 4

Preparing Your House for Sale

Getting your house in tiptop shape and keeping it that way until you sell and move out are critical components of a successful sale. It can make the difference between selling your home and it sitting on the market for months. There are a variety of things you will need to do to prep your home for sale, from cleaning and de-cluttering to repairing and improving. This chapter aims to provide you will a detailed outline of how to go about preparing your home for sale.

A home needs to be prepared inside and out before it is put on the market. Although costly home repairs and renovations are often not necessary to sell a home, you should be prepared to spend some money to add value to your home and get it in the best shape possible to attract buyers. Putting $500 into your house can make the difference between selling it for $157,000 as opposed to

$153,000 and selling in 30 days rather than 90 days, saving you two additional months of house payments.

If you have problems such as serious roof issues or a failing central heat and air system, you will definitely want to fix these issues before you list your house. If you suspect your house may be in need of major repairs, hiring a home inspector to go over the house thoroughly and determine everything that is not functioning properly is a valuable investment. The home inspector will give you an estimate of what the repairs will cost and from there you can determine what repairs you can afford to make. It is always wise to either invest the money to fix major structural issues, or to disclose these issues to any potential buyers. If you do get major repairs done, make sure you hire a licensed professional to do the work.

If your house does not have any major structural issues, like faulty roof, electrical, or plumbing systems, and you have confirmed this with an inspection report, you will want to concentrate on cleaning, de-cluttering, and staging your house. If you have a sense for design, staging your house is fairly easy to do with the help of a few Do's and Don'ts, which will be discussed in detail in Chapter 7. If you are not comfortable with do-it-yourself staging, hiring a decorator is always a great option. The best way to do this is to get a recommendation from a friend, or call a local design firm in your area and ask if they have interior designers. You can also visit **http://topinteriordecorators.com**, which lists interior designers nationally and enables you to search by specific area.

If your house is showing frequently but getting no bids, it generally means you have the house priced correctly for the neighborhood and community but there is a problem with the property itself. It can be that it is out of date, too cluttered, messy, or any number of reasons, but this is usually an indicator that you need to either drop the price or make upgrades and improvements. This is why it is important that the house be in prime showing condition with stylish decoration before potential buyers view it. Assuming you do not need major repairs, some painting, re-arranging furniture, clearing clutter, and so forth can drastically increase the look and appeal of your home.

De-Cluttering

Less is more when showing a house. You are not trying to sell your possessions — you are trying to sell your home. In order to do that, clearing out as many of your personal belongings as possible and opening up all the rooms in your home will enable buyers to envision their own belongings in the space and they will be better able to picture themselves living there.

The first thing you should do is clear all the clutter from your home. It is a distraction; potential buyers are there to see your home, not your belongings. Putting some of your items in storage will not only optimize space and allow buyers to envision themselves living in the home, but it will also keep your belongings safe. You should de-clutter every room in your home, including closets and storage spaces. Below are tips on optimizing space for each room.

The kitchen

The kitchen, along with the bathrooms, is one of the most important rooms in a house to the buyer. A nice, clean, de-cluttered, updated kitchen is much more likely to appeal to a buyer than one that is dirty, outdated, and cluttered with appliances on the countertops. To optimize the space in your kitchen, you should:

- Pull your small appliances off the counter tops and store them in cabinets, or even better, in a storage space in the basement or attic.

- Remove magnets, pictures, and other decorative items from the refrigerator and walls.

- Organize your cabinets, as many people like to open the cabinet doors to see the available space. Be sure to clean and organize the cabinet space and drawers that hold silverware, potholders, and miscellaneous items. If you use throw rugs, be sure they are stylish, in good condition, and free of too much design. Otherwise it is best to remove them altogether. It is also good to have one or two throw rugs in the kitchen, particularly if your kitchen is small.

- Put away your decorative potholders and towels. It is acceptable to keep a minimal amount of hand towels out, but make sure they are not a distracting pattern. It is best if they are one neutral color. If you are using a rug or towel to hide a hole in the wall or a crack in the floor, it is better to repair these.

- Put all your cleaning supplies, including brooms and vacuums, out of sight. Keep them handy but neatly organized in a storage closet or under the sink.

- Clear countertops of miscellaneous things such as keys and mail. Put these neatly in a drawer or a decorative basket on your kitchen table or a shelf.

The bathrooms

Bathrooms are also very important rooms when it comes to selling a home. To de-clutter your bathroom, you should:

- Remove all your personal items, including soaps, shampoo, medications, and cleaning products from the sink top and your shower. Store them neatly in a cabinet for each showing and open house. The goal is to make the shower and sink as clear and clean as possible.

- Remove any towels hanging on your towel racks or behind your door. You only need one nice hand towel hanging in your bathroom.

- Remove all of your throw rugs and toilet lid covers. Toilet lid covers detract from the appeal of the bathroom. Sleek and clean is always the way to go. If you want to keep a rug in the bathroom, purchase an inexpensive neutral-colored one, which will make the bathroom look bigger and cleaner.

Closets and storage

Closets can be challenging to de-clutter because they provide storage. Sellers often underestimate the appeal or lack thereof that a closet can add to a buyer's attraction to a house. A house can be fantastic but if it has lacking or cluttered storage, it can turn off a buyer. Maximize a closet's potential so a buyer can see the possibilities, especially if you have minimal closets in your home. To de-clutter your closets, you should:

- Clear out your storage space of the things you never use and put those things in storage so you have room to put the things you do need regularly in your in-house storage space. Clear your closets of unused items, such as seasonal clothing, and remove any personal items you can. Once you have removed all you can, then organize what is left. Buy more hangers and a shoe rack if you need to.

- For closets in children's rooms that are filled with toys, consider purchasing a toy box or chest to put in the room where you can store the toys instead, which will optimize the space in the closets.

- Expand storage space. You can do this inexpensively by creating an overhead, hanging storage space to provide additional space for storing items. This is an inexpensive fix and will add appeal to the home as buyers always welcome extra storage. You can also get a mobile storage unit delivered to your driveway and keep it there until you move, at which time the company you lease it from will transport the mobile storage unit to your new home, or add shelves to the walls of your garage.

The master bedroom

The master bedroom is also a big selling point for buyers. To declutter your master bedroom, you should:

- Clear out all unnecessary furniture and electronics. If your bedroom doubles as an office, consider moving your office to another space or storing your office equipment and furniture if you can do without it while selling your home. The master bedroom should not have more than a bed, dresser, chest of drawers, and a nightstand. If you have any additional furniture like a desk or chair, remove these if you can to optimize space.

- Clear off all the extra blankets and throws on your bed and keep your bed made at all times that anyone is viewing your home. If you can, keep your bedding to neutral, light colors, which will brighten the room and make it look larger.

- Clear out any throw rugs, especially if you already have carpeting. If you have wooden floors or anything but carpeting, use one at most that is simple and sleek. You do not want anything with too much color or with a bright or loud pattern. People often use throw rugs to hide stained and tattered carpet, but it is always best to fix these before listing your home instead of hiding them. Ultimately, you will have to either make the repair or disclose it to the buyer anyway.

- Remove pictures from your walls and off your furniture if you have a lot of them. This will optimize wall space. It is best to have only one picture or piece of wall décor per wall.

- Clear your knickknacks off your furniture. Put away all books and anything else you normally have sitting on your nightstands or side tables.

- Hide laundry baskets and make sure all your clothing items are put in drawers and hanging neatly in the closet.

The laundry room

The laundry room is not the place to store all the items you have gathered from the de-cluttering process in other rooms. The laundry room, although not the most important room in the house when it comes to appeal, should be free and clear of clutter and organized as much as possible just like any other room. To de-clutter the laundry room, you should:

- Clear out any miscellaneous items you store in the laundry room and consider renting a separate storage space if you have too much stuff to put out of sight.

- Minimize the number of laundry baskets and keep any clothes neatly piled and organized on shelves. Keeping your cleaning supplies in the laundry room is perfectly acceptable, but be sure these are organized in a decorative basket or neatly on a shelf.

The home office

The home office can be another place, in addition to the laundry room, where miscellaneous items are stored. In order to de-clutter your home office, you should:

- Neatly organize all books on your bookshelves and get rid of any books that do not fit on the bookshelves, if you can. Do not leave books on the floor or on bookshelves that are overcrowded.

- Organize paperwork, mail, and other office and computer supplies neatly on your desk.

- Use filing and storage cabinets to store files and extra paperwork, books, or office supplies, but try to keep these out of sight, such as under or behind the desk. Stack these if possible to optimize floor space.

- Clear out all unnecessary décor on the walls, which include plaques, certificates, pictures, and diplomas. Remember, less is more — even in the home office.

- If you have a lot of computer equipment, remove what is used the least. Place electronic cords and wires out of sight by using one outlet, with the help of a surge protector or extension cords. You do not want wires running on the floor from a piece of equipment to an outlet across the room. If you do not have an outlet closer to the equipment, unplug the equipment for showings and hide the cords.

The dining room

The dining room is often one of the easiest rooms to de-clutter because it is not used as often as other rooms in the house. It will still need some attention, however. To de-clutter the dining room, you should:

- Make sure your furniture is not too large for the room. Oftentimes, large china cabinets and dining tables can overpower a dining room. Make sure there is plenty of room to move around. Remove the china cabinet if it overpowers the room. The dining table needs to be the centerpiece of the room and not much else is necessary if the space is small.

- If you have a large table that leaves little room to move around, remove the leaf and store the extra chairs to make more room.

- Remove anything miscellaneous you store in the dining room.

The living room

The living room is one of the first rooms buyers will likely see when they walk through your house, so it is very important you set the de-cluttered tone starting with this room. To de-clutter your living room, you should:

- Organize your furniture the best way it looks in the room. Chapter 7 discusses staging in detail, but just moving around your furniture can optimize space and de-clutter the room.

- Clear out the movies, books, pictures, and knickknacks from your entertainment center as well as the rest of the living room.

- Clear off the fireplace mantle. The fireplace mantle can be a showcase and you want to highlight what beauty it brings to the room with the right décor. Having a few simple candles can highlight the space correctly, but it should be cleared of any pictures, mirrors, or other items.

- If you have an area rug in the room, make sure it is not too bright and that the pattern is not too busy. If it is, consider replacing it with a cheap neutral-colored rug or leaving the hardwood floors bare. If you have carpeting, consider getting rid of all throw rugs if you have any.

The garage

The garage is often underestimated in terms of importance to buyers. Depending on where you live, the garage can be one of the most important parts of the house to a buyer looking for storage and space to park cars. The garage is no longer used only for parking vehicles, but also doubles as a storage area and even a workshop for many families. It is important that it is in as good of showing condition as the living portion of the house.

Garages add to the overall value of the house. An average single-family residence is never built with less than a two-car garage, and quite frequently now they are built with a three-car garage. To de-clutter the garage, you should:

- Clear out anything you store in here that does not fit in built storage space, like boxes. You want the garage to look as big as possible just like the other rooms in your home.

- Move tools and anything else you store in the garage to a designated space so nothing is stacked on the floor or hanging on the walls.

- Move cars to the driveway or street to optimize space and make the garage look larger.

Improvements and Repairs

After you de-clutter your home, the next step is making repairs and improvements. There is a significant difference between making a repair and making an improvement; repairing means fixing something that you already have that needs attention, such as a broken hot water heater, a hole in the wall, or a scratched door. An improvement generally includes an addition to your home, like a pool, bathroom, or brand new roof.

If your home is older and in need of significant repairs, then consider hiring an inspector to review your home and suggest necessary repairs. If you do not want to invest money in making repairs before you list your home, be prepared to disclose that you will be selling the home "As Is," which will mean disclosing all of the issues. You will also likely have to list your home for a lower price than you would if the issues were repaired.

If your home is in good to mint condition and is not in need of any serious repairs, go through each room with the following checklists to ensure that everything is in the best shape possible before you invite potential buyers to view it. Use these checklists for each room in the house.

Doors, windows, walls, and molding

Windows in particular are an important aspect of your home, and ensuring that they work properly will optimize the value of your home, and ultimately yield a higher listing price. Problems with doors, walls, molding, and windows are fairly simple and inexpensive to fix.

Checklist for doors, windows, walls, and molding:

❏ Doors are free of scratches, stains, holes, and cracking
❏ All doors open and close smoothly, without making too much noise
❏ Doorknobs are secured and working properly
❏ Door locks are functioning properly
❏ I know where the keys are to the locks, if there are any
❏ The walls are free of chipping and cracking paint, even behind the doors
❏ The walls and ceiling are free of stains, such as water or paint stains
❏ The molding is firmly attached to the wall
❏ There are no breaks in the molding; it continues around the perimeter of the room
❏ The molding is not chipped, broken, or cracked
❏ There are no gaps between the molding and floor
❏ There are no gaps between the molding and the ceiling
❏ All windows open and close easily
❏ Window locks are functioning properly

❏ Windows are sealed properly and do not leak

❏ Screens are in place and are free or rips and tears

If you could not check off any of the above statements, you will need to make repairs. Most repairs are very simple to make.

> Paint is a great way to not only cover minor stains and discoloring, but it can also neutralize a room. If you have a room painted in a dark or unique color, you may want to consider repainting it a neutral color, such as white or beige, to appeal better to potential buyers. If you have wallpaper up that is old, loudly patterned, or peeling, consider removing it and keeping the walls white. The same goes for children's rooms that are painted or wallpapered in a theme. Buyers usually do not want to have to repaint a home when they move in, and they especially do not want to have to remove wallpaper. Your goal is to create a calm and inviting feel that is neutral; a blank canvas for a potential buyer to come in and make their own.

Countertops, cabinets, and mirrors

Since the condition of the kitchen and bathroom is one of the major selling points of a home, your kitchen and bathroom countertops need to be in good condition for your house to have maximum appeal.

Checklist for countertops, cabinets, and mirrors:

❏ Cabinets open and close properly

❏ Countertops are not stained, chipped, or significantly damaged

❏ Cabinets are free of stains, scratches, and spots

❏ Handles and knobs on cabinets and drawers are secure

❑ There are no handles or knobs missing
❑ Bathroom mirrors are free of cracks

An inexpensive way to give your home a little upgrade is to replace the light and door fixtures, particularly if your current ones are out of date or style. You can find inexpensive door-knobs, light covers, and even chandeliers and other light fixtures at hardware and home improvement stores. OverStock. com, found at **www.overstock.com**, is a great place to shop for discounted items.

Floors

Your floors need to be in tiptop shape for you to get top dollar for your house, especially if you have hardwood floors. Although it is not necessary to replace hardwood floors or carpeting unless they are in very bad condition, you do need to be aware of any flooring issues that result from structural or engineering damage.

Checklist for floors
❑ There are no stains on the carpet
❑ There are no foul odors coming from the carpet
❑ The carpet is not worn in any areas
❑ The carpet is not bunching or coming loose in any areas
❑ There are no carpet tacks exposed
❑ Tiles on the bathroom floor are not stained or cracked
❑ There are no broken or missing tiles
❑ There are no missing boards from my hardwood floors, and no major gaps between boards
❑ Hardwood floors are not dull or worn

Easy Floor Fixes:

If you have various colors of carpet throughout your house, you will want to get it replaced with a new, neutral color that is the same from room to room. While it acceptable if colors vary in the bedrooms slightly, the colors should follow one tone. You do not want carpet in the bathroom. If you have carpet in your bathrooms or kitchen, tear it out and install ceramic tile. Try to avoid the peel-and-stick tile. It is less expensive but it almost always looks cheap. You can also replace carpeting with laminate flooring, which is fairly inexpensive.

There is the option of staining the concrete underneath your flooring once you pull it up. If done well, this can make a house, or at least certain rooms in a house, look fantastic. You can do it yourself if you are handy, or hire someone to do it depending on your budget. Replacing flooring can be expensive, but if it is in bad condition it may be worth it. You can also visit a flooring store to get ideas and then hit the local Habitat for Humanity outlet or builder's outlet for large quantities of leftover or donated materials that may be enough to do a portion of your house. Do not mix and match — if there is not enough available in a store like this then it is best to go where there is enough.

Many times carpet can be stretched and cleaned by a high-quality company and made to look good as new. If your carpet is in very bad shape or very dated in color or style, consider replacing it with a neutral-colored, inexpensive carpet.

Touch'n Foam is an insulating air sealant that can be used to seals cracks in virtually any area of your house and prevent things like moisture and insects from entering through these cracks. The product comes in six different forms depending on which area of your house needs sealing, and can be used to fill everything from small cracks in a window to large holes in the siding of your house. Visit **www.touch-n-foam.com/index.php** for more information and a list of places to purchase.

CASE STUDY: ASK THE BUILDER

Tim Carter
Founder, www.askthebuilder.com
Nationally syndicated newspaper
columnist

*Tim Carter is a nationally syndicated newspaper columnist and founder of **www.AsktheBuilder.com**, an instructional website for do-it-yourself home repairs. The website provides valuable tips and instructional videos on making minor repairs to your home. Below is his advice for making minor home repairs and fixes to prepare your home for sale.*

Problem: Scratched or damaged doors and kitchen cabinets

Solution: Light scratches can be disguised with stain that is applied with a cotton swab. Wipe off any excess stain from adjacent areas immediately. Use a toothpick to carefully apply clear urethane to the scratch only. Deep scratches are nearly impossible to repair without the help of a professional furniture repair person. Equipped with an alcohol lamp and hard lacquer sticks, they can even repair large chips.

Problem: Cracked or crumbling grout

Solution: Dirty grout is best cleaned with oxygen bleach. Oxygen bleach is a non-toxic bleach cleaner that has no fumes, and will not harm colored grout. It works by releasing pure oxygen that can bleach surfaces and remove stains. Before repairing defective grout, clean all the grout and allow it to dry so as to get a perfect color match. Remove all cracked or deteriorating grout carefully so as to not harm the tile. Use hand tools or any number of small power tools like Dremel™ utility tools. Special carbide blades for reciprocating saws are also available. Vacuum out all dust from the crack and install the new grout making sure it is the consistency of firm cake icing.

Problem: Broken or cracked molding

Solution: Use yellow carpenter's glue if possible and clamp the pieces of wood together. If this is not possible, then fill the gap with spackling compound, allow it to dry, and sand it so the profile of the Spackle matches the molding. If the repair is unsatisfactory in appearance, remove the molding and replace with a new piece. Lumber mills can make a new piece to match exactly old profiles.

Problem: Holes or cracks in the wall

Solution: Small holes less than one-quarter inch in diameter can be filled with spackling compound. Large holes should be filled with joint compound or patching plaster. Tape over large holes with drywall tape to prevent cracking around the edges of the hole. Replacing the damaged area with new wallboard can repair very large holes. Tape cracks with drywall tape finishing these areas the same way as you would tape a seam in new drywall. Use dry-setting joint compound on all plaster repairs.

Problem: Molding separating from the wall

Solution: Attempt to nail the molding to the wall by trying to find a wall stud. If this fails, install two nails into the molding within 1 inch of one another with each nail being driven at a 45-degree angle so the tips of the nails are shooting away from each other. The nails act like an expansion anchor. Hold the molding tight to the wall as the nails are being driven. Caulk the crack between the molding and the wall with acrylic caulk.

Problem: Leaking windows

Solution: Look for missing flashing or cracks that need exterior caulk. Replace worn weather stripping to repair air leaks.

Problem: Damaged or worn hardwood floors

Solution: A complete refinishing is usually the only way to get acceptable results. Once the floors look great, apply a maintenance coat of urethane every three to five years so the floors never have to be sanded again.

Problem: Stains on carpets

Solution: Oxygen bleach is perhaps the best carpet cleaner around. It is color safe and will not harm carpet fibers. Mix the powdered oxygen bleach with warm water. Stir until the powder dissolves. Apply the solution to the stain. Allow to soak for ten minutes and pat dry. Removes all stains, including difficult ones like red wine or stains from pets.

Problem: Cracked or buckling tiles in the bathroom

Solution: Remove the damaged tiles carefully and replace any rotten or water-soaked substrate. Use cement board as the new substrate (substrate is a surface that tiles are adhered to). Make sure the surface of the new substrate is in the same plane as the existing. Replace tiles with organic mastic or thinset mortar. Grout the joints and allow to dry 24 hours before placing tile back in service.

Problem: Leaking faucets

Solution: "Replace the cartridge in the faucet body or clean out sediment that may be preventing the faucet to close. Be sure to have a plumber handy in case you are not successful. Never attempt this repair unless you are positive you can have a plumber at your home within an hour. Be sure the water shutoff valve works so you can shut down the water before disassembling the faucet.

Problem: Broken toilet, leaking shower head, and clogged drains

Solution: Always make sure you can shut off the water to the fixture. Toilet tank parts can be repaired with relative ease but replacing an entire toilet is challenging. Chronic clogged drains are usually best cleaned by professionals. Install pipe-thread compound or Teflon tape where showerheads leak at the threaded pipe joint.

Problem: Minor electrical issues, like light switches that do not work, electrical outlets that do not work, exposed wires.

Solution: Never attempt electrical repairs unless you have been trained by a professional on how to make legal repairs. People in the U.S. die each day from electrical fires. Electricity is very dangerous. Simple repairs gone wrong start fires at a later date.

Problem: Broken or missing gutters

Solution: Aluminum gutters can be repaired at joints with special sealants. Be sure aluminum is clean and dry.

Problem: Damaged siding

Solution: Replace damaged siding with new siding. If the siding is wood, paint the new repair piece on all edges and sides before installing it.

Problem: Rotted wood panels

Solution: Small areas of wood rot can sometimes be repaired with wood epoxies. Remove rotted wood and replace with epoxy. Sand to finish, and then paint. Large areas of rot require new wood.

Problem: Oil-stained garage floors and driveways

Solution: Soap and water can remove fresh oil stains. Chemicals are available that can sometimes remove deep, aged oil stains.

Problem: Missing shingles

Solution: Hire a professional roofer to replace shingles. Working on roofs is highly dangerous for a homeowner who has never worked on a sloped roof high off the ground.

Plumbing and plumbing fixtures

The plumbing system includes faucets and toilets in your bathrooms and kitchen. Ensuring these properly function will indicate that your plumbing system is operating correctly and that there are no major repairs that need to be made. If you suspect there is a larger issue with your plumbing system, enlist the help of a home inspector. A home inspector may not look at the condition of your carpet or the color of your paint, as those are not issues of function. They will check to see that the plumbing, electrical, and things of that nature are in good working order.

Checklist for plumbing:

- ❏ All toilets are flushing and refilling properly
- ❏ Toilets are securely attached to the floor
- ❏ Seals around toilets and faucets are secure
- ❏ The faucet does not leak
- ❏ There are no cracks, chips, or breaks on the faucet, handles, or toilet
- ❏ Shower doors open and close properly
- ❏ The shower and shower head do not leak water
- ❏ Drains work properly and are not clogged
- ❏ Tiles in the shower are not breaking, cracking, or buckling
- ❏ Caulking in the shower is still in place and not cracking

If there are no serious leaks coming from underneath anything, these repairs are fairly easy to make. Anything that is chipped or broken should be replaced as well as loose and broken tiles. Though a home inspector will find any serious leaks, it is better if you try to spot and repair these first. Waiting for a home inspector to identify the problem may result in you having to hire someone to repair it, which costs you more money. Often, buyers want repairs to be made by a licensed professional, but a leaky faucet can be repaired by a handy homeowner if the problem is not too serious.

Clog removers are a simple and easy solution to fix clogged drains and it can be purchased at virtually any grocery or hardware store. Simply follow the directions on the back of the bottle but if you suspect the clog needs professional attention, call a plumber.

Electrical

Building codes and requirements have changed drastically over the years for safety reasons. Depending on whether your buyer is getting a government- or FHA-insured loan, your electrical system could come under heavy scrutiny not only by a home inspector, but also by an appraiser. If you live in an older home and your electrical system has not been updated, you may find yourself with a problem after the home has been inspected.

Checklist for electrical system

❑ All light switches are properly working
❑ All outlets are working properly and none are shorted (usually indicated by black stains or marks around the plug in)
❑ All switches in the breaker box are correctly labeled
❑ There are not exposed wires around light fixtures or outlets
❑ GFIs (ground-fault circuit interrupters) are properly working

Although you should leave most electrical problems to a certified electrician, if you are confident that a certain electrical problem is minor, such as an outlet that is not working, visit "The Circuit Detective: Homeowners' Resource for Electrical Troubleshooting" for help and answers to common electrical problems. The website is located at **www.thecircuitdetective.com**.

Electrical problems are best left to a certified electrician. If you have a question as to the condition of the wiring in your house, you should have it checked by an electrician. If any repairs are called for, it is usually required by the city government that only a licensed electrician make any needed repairs.

Heat, air systems, and hot water tanks

Responsible homeowners do regular maintenance on central heat and air systems as well as air conditioner units, usually before the season begins when the systems will be running for several months, to ensure they are in good working order. If these systems have not been kept up to date, you will want to call a licensed professional to inspect the functionality of the systems. Serious central heat and air issues can hinder a sale and would be better repaired in advance of a home inspection.

A home inspector, though valuable to the process, knows a little about a lot. He or she is trained to look for indicators of problems, not necessarily to know exactly what the problem is. If he or she finds a fault with central heat and air system, though it may not be anything serious, it could alarm the buyers unnecessarily.

Checklist for your heating and cooling systems

- ❏ Window air conditioner units are clean and free of debris
- ❏ The filters for my window units have been changed in the past six months
- ❏ The hot water tank is free of leaks and is not worn out in any area

If you do not know what to look for or are uncomfortable making these repairs on your own, it is always best to call a professional.

Even if you have an older home that does not have energy efficient appliances, you can still save on heating and cooling costs and demonstrate this to any potential buyers with a few simple strategies. According to the U.S. government's Energy Star website for national energy conservation efforts, **www.energystar.gov**, doing minor things like the following can save valuable time and energy:

- Insulate the first few feet of the pipes connected to your hot water heater.

- Lower the temperature of your hot water heater to 120 Fahrenheit.

- Every three months, remove one quart of water from your hot water tank to remove any build up that prevents your heater from working properly.

- Be sure to check with the manufacturer of your hot water heater before making any repairs.

Cleaning Your House

Now that you have cleared out the clutter and made your repairs, it is time to clean. Making sure your house is clean is perhaps one of the most important things you can do to maximize its appeal. You can make repairs and improvements, list your house at the right price, and do all the right marketing but if your house is dirty, you significantly reduce the attractiveness to the buyer.

It is very important that you pay attention to every detail when it comes to cleaning your house. Keep in mind that you have lived there for a while and may have grown accustomed to the stains on the shower tile, but buyers may be turned off by something like this. What was made to shine should shine.

The kitchen and bathrooms

Kitchen

In the kitchen, this mostly applies to faucets, sinks, and any stainless steel appliances and fixtures. Clean and remove all stains, watermarks, and fingerprints with a mild cleanser designed for stainless steel use, which you can find at most hardware and home supply stores. Water stains, in particular, are common on faucets, so you will need to clean these areas often — probably before each open house and showing to keep it spotless.

If you have an older sink with deeper stains you may need a more advanced cleanser. Use a scrubber to rid stains on sinks and faucets — be sure to penetrate the surface with micro-scrubbers to remove deep-set stains. You can also use this product on bathtubs, sinks, and walls to remove deep-set stains you cannot manage to remove with a milder cleanser.

Clean the cabinets, and if they do not need repairs, consider painting or staining them if they look worn. If they are just in need of some polishing, use a product that is specific to your cabinet's material. If your cabinets are wooden, for instance, use a wood-based polisher to remove dust, fingerprints, and mild stains.

Commonly Used Cleaning Products:

Be sure to use the appropriate cleaning product for each surface.

Surface	Best Cleaning Product or Solution
Wood furniture and cabinets	Pledge®
Wood floors	Murphy® Oil Soap
Granite or stone	Hot water and a sponge will clean most surface stains, but a granite cleaner like Method® Granite and Marble Cleaner is good for tougher stains.
Porcelain	Barkeeper's Friend or Cameo for tough stains on porcelain sinks and tubs; ¼ cup of vinegar in 2 gallons of hot water for porcelain floors.
Stainless Steel	Club soda, olive oil, or eucalyptus oil can be applied directly to stainless steel to remove stains. Stainless steel cleaners like Cerama Bryte® are good for removing deep stains on appliances.
Carpeting	For set stains, do not use soap to clean. Use products that do not contain soap like Woolite® OxyDeep Spot and Stain Carpet Cleaner. Visit The Carpet and Rug Institute at **www.carpet-rug.org** for other product recommendations and cleaning tips.
Glass	Windex® or Method Blue Sky Glass Cleaner
Mirrors	Windex, or mix 1 tablespoon of regular dish soap with warm water and wipe with a microfiber cloth.
Outside furniture	Windex Outdoor All-in-One Streak Free Shine

Additionally, all your appliances should be cleaned thoroughly — this includes the inside of your oven, the oven vent, the boiler, and the shelves and drawers in the refrigerator. A place that is often neglected is behind the cook top where grease and food is splattered. If you can, pull your oven out a few inches and clean the wall behind the oven and the floor. Clean the inside and top of the vent hood. It takes no time at all for a distasteful layer of dust and grease to settle there. If you have a built-in microwave over your cook top, clean underneath the microwave and remove the glass plate in the microwave to clean.

Thoroughly sweep and mop your floors each time you have an open house or showing. If the floor grout is dirty and stained, you might want to consider getting a small steamer to clean the grout and then reseal it to prevent further staining — or you can purchase grout seal at any hardware store. If you cannot afford to reseal the grout either for time or money reasons, you can use oxygen bleach to clean some of the dirt from the grout in between tiles. This will not make your floors look brand new, but will lift a few layers of dirt to significantly lighten the coloring of the grout and bring it back to its natural color.

Bathrooms

In your bathrooms, make sure mirrors are cleaned thoroughly with a non-streak cleaner. You will want to wipe the mirrors each time you host an open house or showing, as mirrors often tend to get streaky. Next, clean off all the buildup around the base of the faucet and the faucet and handles, using the appropriate cleaner. Use a grout cleaner like oxygen bleach to gently remove dirt and stains from your floor if it is tiled.

In the tub or shower, do the same for the grout. Remove stains from the sinks, tubs, tile floors, and showers. If you have an older bathtub that is chipping or peeling, consider getting it re-glazed, refinished, or installing an acrylic liner. Re-glazing is fairly inexpensive and typically lasts about three to five years before it begins chipping again. Either method will greatly improve the appearance of a chipping bathtub.

When you clean, clear everything off counters, sink tops, and other surfaces so you clean the entire surface and not just around items on the space. This way, if things need to be moved during the staging process, you will not have to worry about certain areas being dirty, or about cleaning and dusting again.

The rest of the house

The kitchen and bathrooms are the most important rooms when it comes to selling a house, and they also happen to be the hardest to clean. Once you have cleaned, de-cluttered, and repaired these rooms, the rest is easy.

Throughout the rest of the house, including the living room, dining rooms, laundry room, home office, entryways, bedrooms, and closets, dusting and vacuuming are very necessary. All wood furniture, shelves, cabinets, and other surfaces should be thoroughly dusted. Open cabinets and drawers in your entertainment center, tables, and hutch, and dust inside. Use a ladder for hard-to-reach places like the top of a hutch or entertainment center and make sure to dust up there. For awkward spaces like corners and crevices, use a duster with an extendable handle. The product is great for dusting hard-to-reach spaces.

Shelf paper adds a layer of protection to your shelves and cabinets that will prevent at least some stains, dirt, and nicks. It will also add some color and character to your space and can brighten up darker cabinet spaces. Choose a solid, neutral color to line your shelves and drawers. You can find shelf paper at most home supply and hardware stores.

Small spaces like entranceways, basements, laundry rooms, pantries, and breakfast nooks should not be neglected. Be sure to dust, organize, and clean in these spaces as well; you never know where a potential buyer will explore during an open house.

One of the first things people see when they walk up to your home, or drive by it, is the front door, which makes it one of the most important aspects of your home. The front door makes the critical first impression, and provides a sneak peek into what the rest of the house is like. The front door's condition can indicate what kind of shape the rest of the house is in, and if you neglect to include your door in your cleaning and repairing routine, it may send the wrong message to buyers.

If you have a glass storm door, be sure to clear it of fingerprints, streaks, and water stains. If you have a screen door, clear off dust and pollen with a vacuum, using the hose with a soft brush. Be sure the locks on both your storm or screen door and your front door work properly and that all the hinges are tightened. Naturally, you should do the same for your back door, and any side doors you have to your home. If any screens are ripped or torn, consider replacing just the screen part or removing this part of the door altogether. It is not uncommon for a home to have just a front door without a screen; many buyers actually prefer this, particularly for a front door.

Outside of the house

The garage
The garage is a very important aspect of a home when it comes to selling, as it provides storage space for cars, tools, toys, furniture, luggage, and countless miscellaneous items. Because it is not just a place to store cars, the garage should be as well maintained as the rest of your home to be the most appealing to buyers.

Assuming you have de-cluttered already, consider power washing the floor of your garage to remove all oil, grease, and paint stains. A power washer is fairly inexpensive to rent and can improve the condition and aesthetics of the garage floor. Painting your floor is an option to consider if it is in really bad shape or if it is cracking. Epoxy — a tough, long-lasting coating or floor paint — can be used over concrete to prevent grease and other stains. Although the process can be tedious, the paint comes in a variety of colors and can improve your floors and prevent future stains. If you have minor cracking, you may want to seal those cracks first using a sealant or flexible epoxy and then use the paint. However, paining over minor cracks will not be damaging. The epoxy paint will probably cover these cracks if they are small enough. Most hardware stores carry epoxy paint.

Sealing cracks on your garage floor is fairly easy. First, make sure the cracks are not an indication that there is a problem with your house's foundation. If you are unsure, the best thing to do is to hire a civil engineer to confirm your foundation is sound. If the cracks are not foundation-related, use an epoxy crack sealer or similar product, like CrackWeld Floor Repair, before you paint. Clean all debris out of the cracks and follow the sealer instructions. Wait 48 hours — or longer, depending on the instructions — to paint over the sealant.

The front yard

Like the front door, the outside of your home will be the first thing potential buyers see when they pull up for an open house or drive by your home. Therefore, the outside of your home should be as clean, maintained, and orderly as the inside. Start by going around your home and picking up any trash in the landscaping, bushes, and yard. If you are a smoker, be sure to get all the cigarette butts in the yard as well. Remove all knickknacks and decorations, including ceramic animals and signs. You really only need some basic lawn furniture and perhaps your grill and a fire pit on the porch.

Next, clean the outside of your windows using a ladder to reach tall windows. Wash the outside of the windows, and remember the outside glass will undoubtedly be dirtier than the inside. If you can do it yourself, clean out the gutters and clear away leaves and other debris from your landscaping and lawn.

If you have children, clear out any toys on the lawn, including plastic swing sets and other toys that can be moved. Remove any furniture on your lawn and remove all furniture on your patio or deck, if you have one, besides a table and chairs, umbrella, and a few additional pieces if you have a larger patio area. If you have tables and chairs scattered around the patio or deck, tucked or stacked in corners, clear these out and put them in storage. It is best to have the lawn and patio or deck as clear as possible to optimize space.

> Clean your screen doors and windows to make your entryways and windows look fresher. To clean your screens, remove them and place them on a surface you are comfortable getting wet, like a driveway. Take a broom and sweep the screens in all directions to remove dust.

Next, you should consider power washing your deck, patio, sidewalks, driveway, and any other concrete area on your property. Particularly if you are putting your home on the market in the spring and live in a four-season climate, you will want to clear out all the debris and leaves that accumulated in these areas over the winter. If you have siding, you should also power wash that.

If you have a brick home and the bottom bricks have become stained and dirty, power washing the bricks can make them look much cleaner. If you do not own a power washer, you can rent one from a hardware store or equipment-leasing store — it is well worth the time and cost invested.

Value-added improvements

It may be necessary to make improvements to your house depending on its condition. If your house is very old, it will likely be necessary to invest time and money to making some improvements.

Not all improvements will add value to your home and not all are necessary. Even if you spend $30,000 to completely remodel your outdated kitchen and bathrooms, you may not automatically be able to list your home for $30,000 more.

If something in your house is in need of repair or replacement, such as your hot water heater, central air conditioning system, roof, electrical and plumbing systems, consider enlisting the services of a professional roofer or Heating, Ventilation, and Air Conditioning (HVAC) specialist to do an inspection and fix any repairs that need immediate attention. This will enable you to ensure potential buyers you have had older aspects of your home inspected and repaired. The investment to pay a professional will pay off in the end if you have an older home as it will reassure the buyers that things are in proper working order.

Your house may look spectacular with $30,000 invested in it, but there may be a house down the block that has the same updates. You will undoubtedly be able to list your home for significantly more than what you would have had to list it for before the upgrades, but you are still subjected to the demand of the market. Making the $30,000 in improvements may simply enable you to compete price-wise with newer homes in your neighborhood.

There *are* improvements you can make that will add more value to your house than what you paid for the improvement. In general, improvements to bathrooms and the kitchen yield the largest value while pools yield the least. If your house is more than 15 to 20 years old and still has the original kitchen, bathrooms, roof, and water heater, you should consider improving these areas to get your optimal sale price. This does not mean you need to invest tens of thousands of dollars to renovate your house from top to bottom, but you will want to invest a few thousand making some improvements that will add value to your house. In fact, depending on market demand and other homes in your area, it could be more valuable to make just a few improvements rather than renovating an entire kitchen.

Improvements that will increase the value of your house include:

- **Kitchen:** Replacing the cabinets and old appliances with new ones instead of renovating the entire kitchen

- **Roofing:** Replacing broken shingles instead of getting a whole new roof, but be sure to disclose the condition of your roof to your buyer

- **Bathrooms:** Replacing cabinets, faucet fixtures, and lighting instead of replacing everything like the floor, bathtub, and tiling

- **Heating System:** There is not much you can do to improve an old water heater except disclose this to your buyer instead of purchasing a new one. Installing a new one will not add significant value

- **Flooring:** Replace missing or worn floorboards, polish, and re-finish hardwood floors; shampoo carpets instead of replacing entire floor

The following improvements will add the most value to your house. These values are very general and are subjective to the real estate market in your local area.

Improvement	Approximate Cost	Approximate Value Added
Upgraded kitchen and bathrooms	$1,500 to $2,000	$3,000 to $4,000
Painting, inside and out	$500 to $1,500	$1,500 to $2,000
Landscaping	$300 to $600	$1,500 to $2,000
Updating plumbing and electrical systems	$300 to $600	$1,000 to $1,500
Repairing floors and carpeting	$500 to $1,000	$1,500 to $2,000

According to HomeGain (**www.homegain.com**), an online resource for Realtors and homeowners selling a house, the biggest value in improvement is cleaning and de-cluttering your house. It is important to determine a budget before you begin the selling process. This way, you will be able to determine what you can afford to do in terms of improvements and repairs and what you cannot afford to do. Knowing this will determine a more accurate listing price for your house. Make necessary repairs and select improvements *before* you put your home on the market to maximize your potential listing price and avoid delays due to repairs the inspector requests.

Chapter 5

Determining Your Price

Pricing is perhaps the most important aspect of selling your house. Listing your home for a reasonable, competitive price can mean the difference between selling your house and having it sit on the market for months with no bids. There are a variety of factors to consider in addition to those discussed in previous chapters, such as demand, the condition of your local real estate market, and the location and condition of your house. The comparative market analysis (CMA) and an appraisal play a key role in determining the right listing price for your house.

Getting an Appraisal

One of the first questions sellers often ask when getting ready to sell their home is: "Do I need to get an appraisal?" The answer is: not necessarily. Getting an appraisal — which will cost about

$300 to $350 — is a great way to determine an accurate price for your home. This appraisal is optional and different from the appraisal that will be done through your buyer's lender further along in the process.

An appraiser will do a complete evaluation of your home and determine an appraised value based on your home's condition, location, and the CMA of houses that sold in your neighborhood. The benefit of having an appraisal is finding out what your home is worth before you put it on the market. This can save you time in the long run if you price too high and then realize after the house has been on the market for a few months and is not selling that your house is not worth as much as you thought. Since the buyer's lender will order an appraisal as well, it is beneficial to have one on your own and be prepared.

On the negative side, appraisers tend to appraise homes for a lower value than what you may be able to get for the house mainly because they are not 100 percent familiar with the demands of the local real estate market in your specific neighborhood. For example, an appraiser may estimate your house is worth $250,000, but you know some of the other homes in your neighborhood have sold for $265,000. The appraiser often does not take into consideration the economics of your immediate community and would not consider, for instance, the availability of employment in the area. Because of these factors, the appraiser's estimate should be taken as one factor in a pool of factors to consider when pricing your house.

If you cannot afford an appraisal or prefer not to get one, it is possible to effectively price your house based on a comparative market analysis (CMA). This is what a Realtor would do to determine an accurate listing price for your home, and getting a CMA is fairly easy to do on your own.

CASE STUDY:
PRO FSBO SELLERS

Mike and Amanda Karfakis

Amanda Karfakis and her husband, Mike, decided to put their home on the market in June 2009. Despite the volatility of the market at that time and the pessimistic economic situation, the Karfakises placed their home on the market without an agent in an effort to save money. They had previously bought two buildings for business purposes without the help of an agent, and figured that given their experience they had a good chance at being successful in selling on their own.

The Karfakises approached the marketing process aggressively, and used all the resources they had at their fingertips to spread the word about their home. "Before we even put the 'For Sale' sign out, we started telling our neighbors the house was going up for sale. This started a buzz in the neighborhood. We also created highly professional signage for the door and window along with a take-away flier container. Each sign displayed a dedicated website address that detailed the property in full along with lots of photos," Amanda said.

Because the Karfakises had a plan and created a strategy before they placed their home on the market, they successfully closed on the deal within 30 days of listing their home for sale — an impressive feat considering the market conditions. Equally impressive was their ability to settle on a price they were happy with. "We had the property priced competitively at $245,000," Amanda said. "Similar houses were on the market for $250,000 and $260,000 and they just weren't getting sold. We knew our property had some limitations, like one small bathroom and no closets in the bedrooms. We were willing to negotiate down to $234,000 as our lowest price. We ended up selling the house for $234,000, so we were $11,000 below the asking price. We were satisfied with the sale price and profit we were able to make from the house. It was worth every part of the negotiation down from our asking price."

During the process, a friend of theirs who happened to be a Realtor approached them about listing the home with him. "One Realtor contacted us, but it was a friend who knew we were putting the property up for sale. He wanted a commission for the sale, and we just couldn't justify a commission for something we could handle on our own. We couldn't see the point in paying someone thousands of dollars when we were quite capable of showing the property and negotiating the deal on our own," Amanda said.

In order to be successful in selling your home on your own, the Karfakises suggest a number of things. First, know the market in your area by reviewing recent home sales. Know your lowest possible number for the home. As for pricing, list the home to sell — about 10 to 25 percent below market value if you want it to sell quickly. Additionally, know that you can always list the home in the MLS for around $400. A buyer's agent can still see the listing, yet you will save up to 3.5 percent by keeping a listing agent away from the table. Know that without the MLS, you will have to market heavily to get the property seen and visited by prospective buyers. If you do not offer an agent's fee, agents probably will not want to show the house to their clients.

Amanda also suggested listing your home on Craigslist because people really do look there for houses. When you write the listing, consider offering an agent's fee, like 2.5 percent or more. This way, agents of prospective buyers will be more likely to show the house. The Karfakises also created a Web page for the house. For them, it was easy because they own a branding agency, with designers on staff who created a one-page website quickly.

Finally, Amanda suggests taking friends through the house before you put it on the market, "So they can tell you what stands out as nice — or not so nice," she said. "Fix those not-so-nice things before you start showing the house to prospective buyers. Tell everyone you know and meet that you're selling your house. Word of mouth goes a long way and word travels quickly."

For Amanda and her husband, the most challenging part of the process was negotiating with the buyers. "The hardest part was playing the game of negotiation, but overall it wasn't that tough because we priced the house to sell and the buyer knew he was getting a great deal," she said. "Therefore, both parties knew where to draw the line in terms of negotiation. This made the negotiating a lot easier."

Overall, the process went very smoothly for the Karfakises. In the future, Amanda and her husband look forward to selling FSBO again. "We would absolutely do an FSBO again," Amanda said. "I don't know that we will ever use an agent. The entire process was smooth and comfortable for us."

Getting a Comparative Market Analysis

A comparative market analysis, or CMA, is a report detailing the value of similar properties in your geographical area in terms of size and condition. The report is essentially an analysis of the sale prices of these properties and will give you an idea of what similar homes in your area sold for and therefore, what they are worth.

The best way to get a CMA is from a Realtor. Even though you are not giving the Realtor the listing, many agents will offer to do a CMA for free for you in hopes that you will decide to list with them. Make sure that you do not sign any sort of contract that obligates you to list with a Realtor if he or she completes a CMA for you. If you prefer not to involve a Realtor, completing a CMA on your own is fairly simple. You can get this information by visiting your county courthouse online or in person and researching property records. Assuming your county is good about keeping the information updated, you should get fairly accurate information.

When it comes to using a CMA, it is important that you are comparing to properties that are in fact similar to yours. For the most part, include homes from your own neighborhood that have a similar square footage and number of bedrooms and bathrooms, for instance, and exclude the ones that are obviously not comparative to yours. If you include homes that are significantly different than yours, either in size, location, or condition, you may not be getting the most accurate idea of what your home is worth.

Ideally, a good CMA will include five properties that have sold within the last year that are within 100 square feet in size of yours and built within a few years of yours. You also want to stick with properties that have the same number of bedrooms and bathrooms. If your house has a three-car garage, then you want to compare with other homes with three-car garages. It is important that your comparables have been sold within the last six months and definitely no longer than a year ago.

Some Realtors will try to get you to list your house with them by using houses that are not comparable to yours in your CMA — they may do this to demonstrate how much more effective they would be in getting you a higher price for your house by using houses that sold for a higher price in your neighborhood. If you get a CMA from a Realtor, look over the report and make sure the houses included are similar to yours in size, condition, and location.

If you cannot find five homes within a few blocks of your home, then expand your search to within 1 square mile of your home as long as the homes are similar to yours in terms of square footage, condition, and number of bathrooms and bedrooms. If you have difficulty finding enough homes with the exact number of bedrooms and bathrooms, then you can include homes with one more or less but you will need to adjust the value depending on whether your house has one more or one less bedroom or bathroom than the house you are using for comparison.

Below is a sample of a simple CMA.

	Address	Bedrooms	Baths	Square Ft.	Garage	List Price	Sale Price	Date Sold
	COMPARABLE MARKET ANALYSIS							
S	1212 Fifth St.	4	2	1804	Y	$153,500		
1	1000 Fifth St.	4	2	1788	N	$147,500	$145,000	11/18/15
2	1600 Fourth St.	4	2	1896	Y	$152,900	$152,000	02/05/15
3	1340 Second St.	4	2.5	1912	N	$149,950	$149,950	05/06/15
4	1100 Ninth St.	4	2	1692	N	$145,000	$142,750	12/31/14
5	1440 Fourth St.	4	2	1692	N	$154,000	$152,000	8/31/15

Average List Price: $149,870
Average Sale Price: $148,340
Average Sq. Ft: 1796
Average Sale per Sq. Ft: $82.59

In this example chart, 1212 Fifth St. is the subject property. The properties you are comparing with will be listed next.

This example contains five comparable properties — all with the same number of bedrooms as the subject property, and all but one have the same number of bathrooms. None of the properties, including the subject property, have a garage with the exception of one home. As you can see in this sample CMA, the home with a garage sold for slightly more than the ones without with the exception of the last home on the CMA. It sold at the same price as the one with a garage, perhaps because it was in good condition and needed fewer repairs and changes than the other homes on this report.

As you can see, the square footage on all the comparable properties is close to the same as the subject property. This is important because your property will ultimately be priced based on a price per square foot. If you hire an appraiser, he or she will appraise your home based on its square footage. In this example, the five comparable properties sold for an average price per square foot of $82.59. The average price per square footage on homes sold in your area will be the basis for your price. Take your square footage and multiply the average price per square foot, and you have a good sales price for your home.

> To determine a price per square foot, divide the sales price by the square footage of the home. If you take the square footage of your home and multiply the average price per square foot, you will have a good sales price for your home.

Based on this number, you may choose to list your home slightly higher than average if you have additional features in your home that would add to the value, such as a fire place, or if your home is in better condition than the others. However, it is important to be objective in your evaluation.

A CMA can also help you determine how long it will take for your home to sell. To determine this, take each of your comparable properties and the number of days each one was on the market, total the days of all the comparables, and divide that number by the number of comparable properties you have in your CMA. This number is your average length of time on the market. To determine your suggested selling price, take the average selling price per square foot, multiply your square footage by $82.59, and you have a suggested price of $153,500. This is the average selling price for homes in your area.

Armed with this information you not only can be better prepared, but you can also determine if you want to adjust the price either lower or higher than the average sales price.

A CMA may not be as useful to you when there are not enough homes to serve as comparables in your area. For example, if your home is on a large piece of land, perhaps in a rural area, it may be some distance away from other properties. Your property also may be very unique compared to surrounding properties and houses. In this case, getting an appraisal on the property would be necessary to enable you to price it right.

Similarly, your home may have additional features, like a swimming pool, that will add some value to your home compared to those similar homes on your CMA that do not have pools. In general, swimming pools do not add as much value to a home as they cost to install. If, for example, you have installed a $30,000 swimming pool in the backyard, you will probably not be able to add $30,000 to the sales price and expect to sell it for that price. You may get an additional percentage of that $30,000, but you likely will not get the price back that you put into the pool. The amount of money you would get back from installing a pool is greatly dependent on where you live, but in general you can expect to make 50 percent or less of your investment in a pool.

The issue with a swimming pool is that most people do not want a pool in many parts of the country. In areas that experience four seasons, like New York, having a pool is not a necessity and may actually hinder a property's value. Many people do not want the hassle of taking care of a pool, particularly in off-season months, and many buyers would prefer having the yard space as opposed to a swimming pool.

The good news, however, is that buyers who are looking specifically for a pool will be more inclined to your home if your home has one. It is oftentimes hard for a buyer to find all the features they are looking for in addition to a pool.

There may be other features to your home that you may think will add more value than they actually do. You may have an extra half-lot, for instance, than other homes in your area with the same basic features. Even though you have extra land, the land may not be ideal for building and adding to the property. One half-lot is not enough land to build another house on, and assuming you live in a neighborhood with standard city ordinances and restrictions, it is unlikely a buyer would be able to use this land for animals, for instance. At best, a buyer could possibly build a shed or garage on the land, so the land will ultimately not add much value to your home. Unless a buyer is specifically looking for an extra half-lot, it will not add much more to your asking price.

What determines your house's value

The status of the national market and the economy will have a major impact on your home's value; however, your local market will dictate your home's value more specifically. You may be in an area where prices are on the rise. Or, you may be in an area where home values are starting to cool off just a bit after the post-2008 real estate boom. Remember, the market can vary from one small suburban city to the neighboring city, which further underlines the importance of doing a comparative market analysis.

A common strategy for determining a home's value is researching your home's value in your county court house records. The county assessor determines the value for tax purposes, but it often has little to do with what your house can sell for. Typically, taxes are determined by multiplying the tax rate by your property's assessed value. Property tax rates, how these taxes are determined, and how your house is assessed and valued for tax purposes vary widely not only by state, but by county. For example, Long Island, New York, is divided into two counties: Nassau and Suffolk. Nassau County taxes are significantly higher than taxes in Suffolk County even though the two counties border each other.

A home can also be reflected in the court records incorrectly, perhaps with an inaccurate square footage, or the wrong lot size. It is also common that areas of your home are documented as living space, like an attic, when in fact the space is not livable. These inaccuracies result from dated methods used for tracking and keeping information, as well as the fact that assessors generally come around once a year at the most to assess the property and a lot can happen to value in a year's time.

In general, you will want to take the CMA, appraisal, court records, number of foreclosures in your area, number of homes on the market, and general market status into consideration when pricing your home. All of these factors must be considered to appropriately price your home.

You can also get valuable help by visiting one of these top websites used by professionals in the real estate industry:

- Value My House: **www.valuemyhouse.com** — If you complete a request form, a VMH professional will prepare an electronic report for you. You can also browse through houses for sale.

- Home Gain: **www.homegain.com** — On this website, you can find a Realtor, search house values and prices, and search for houses for sale.

Pricing Tips

One of the biggest mistakes FSBO sellers make is pricing their homes too high. If you want to sell quickly and attract multiple offers, price just below the market. Why would a buyer choose someone else's 3-bedroom, 2-bathroom down the block from you home listed at $279,000 when your 3-bedroom, 2-bathroom home is listed at $269,500?

Knowing your neighborhood

One of the most important aspects of pricing your home is what your neighborhood is like, which includes school systems, property taxes, and the general community vibe. It is important to you know your neighborhood and community for two reasons: it helps with determining a price, and it helps with marketing.

You should know about the quality of the school systems in your neighborhood, how close you are to shopping areas, how close you are to highways and other thoroughfares, what services are available to the community, and other similar facts. One of the biggest factors in a buyer's decision to purchase a home is the quality of the school system. If you live in a great school district, then you want to be sure to market that as a positive factor. For the most part, you can expect that buyers will already know the quality of the school system in your neighborhood, and many of them will be looking in your area because of it.

Another significant factor for buyers is the proximity of your home to work. If you live close to a military base or other large employer, then you will want to include that information on your fliers and in your ads. Your flier might read, "Ten minutes from Tinker Air Force Base."

If your community offers something special or unique like a great community pool or dog park, include that as well. All of these can add a little value to your house and a lot of value to the buyer's motivation to buy in your area. Additionally, you will want to know how the traffic flows around your neighborhood. This is valuable, because you can determine where there is high traffic, such as major intersections for car traffic and busy shopping areas for foot traffic, and can place your signs in those places.

Another important fact to consider when pricing your home is the amount of foreclosures in your neighborhood. You could be competing with foreclosure homes in your neighborhood, although many of the buyers who purchase foreclosed homes are investors and have the large amounts of cash necessary to bid on these homes. Buyers looking at your house are likely buyers looking for a new house as opposed to an investment property looking to produce an income, so you will not be competing with foreclosure homes in this sense.

If there are a high number of houses in foreclosure in your neighborhood, however, buyers may be skeptical of the neighborhood. Some people are not so sure about moving to an area where the quality of the neighborhood may be declining due to abandoned and foreclosed properties. Having knowledge of your community helps you have realistic expectations and market your property effectively.

Sizing up the competition

Other homes for sale in your neighborhood can have both a positive and a negative impact on your own listing. If there are too many homes on the market in your area, buyers may be turned off because the neighborhood may seem too transient. Additionally, buyers have many options in a market where many houses are for sale, and that could naturally slow your ability to sell. On the positive side, traffic in the general areas will increase because of other houses for sale and the marketing of those houses.

Traffic will increase in your neighborhood particularly if houses in the area are listed with a Realtor, because most homes listed with an agent are listed on a Multiple Listing Service (MLS). The service, which you can find at **www.mls.com**, is a national database of all houses listed by local MLS sites, represented by a Realtor or real estate professional. There is an option on the website to search foreclosed, bank-owned, or FSBO listings as well. If there are many houses in your area listed on MLS through a Realtor, it is likely that buyers looking for houses in your neighborhood on MLS will come across your listing as well. Houses on the market in your area listed with a Realtor also draw traffic to the general vicinity, increasing the chance that these buyers will be exposed to your FSBO advertising.

Similarly, houses represented by a real estate agent in your area can yield you important traffic for your open house. You can capitalize on the resources they are using to drive traffic into the neighborhood and hold your open house on the same day. The benefit to you is twofold: you save some money on marketing by taking advantage of theirs and you get extra exposure from buyers who are coming to their open houses or to view the houses they have listed.

In real estate, timing is important. If you are not in a rush to put your house on the market, then taking a few weeks to observe the real estate activity in your neighborhood will be beneficial for getting a sense of your local market. Depending on the size of your neighborhood, it is ideal to list when there are other properties listed with a good percentage of them listed with a Realtor. Neighborhood home sales tend to go in cycles; a particular neighborhood may go a year or two with not much for sale and then suddenly one summer, several go up for sale. Try to list when there are neither too many nor too few houses for sale. Note the listing prices for these houses; this information will help you in pricing your home.

Chapter 6

Listing Your Home

After you have made any necessary repairs to your house and determined a price, it is time to put it on the market. Before you do this, it is important that you get yourself organized. You should have a game plan in place for the whole selling process to help you keep up with your marketing, phone calls, showings, and open houses. It is also important to have a strategy in place for not only marketing and advertising, but also handling paperwork and the closing.

There are a variety of strategies you can take when it comes to listing your home. Nearly 80 percent of people looking for homes begin their search on the Internet. Therefore, listing your home on the Internet is almost a necessity, in addition to using signs and fliers around your neighborhood. You must also consider whether you are going to use a discount brokerage, like Assist-2-Sell, or if you are going to offer a commission to a buyer's agent as an incentive to bring potential buyers to see your house.

What You Need to Stay Organized

Here is a list of items you can purchase (if you do not already have them) to help you stay on track and organized through the selling process:

- A "Phone Calls Received" logbook from an office supply store, or a legal pad that is used for keeping track of phone calls you have received, whether you spoke with the caller or need to call her back, the caller's contact information, and the outcome of the conversation.

- A folder to keep fliers so you are ready to replace them when needed. Keep this with you when you are out so if you are near a place with a cork or display board for fliers, you have them handy and can place one up for people to see.

- An open house logbook that asks for name, phone number, and e-mail address to help you keep up with open house traffic and follow up with potential buyers to inform them of price drops or other information about your home. You can also make an open house logbook by purchasing a notebook and making yourself a page on the computer that requests this information.

- Tacks to keep on hand for hanging fliers wherever the opportunity presents itself.

- Printer paper for fliers and other marketing material.

- Plenty of ink for your printer.

- A digital camera for taking pictures for your fliers and internet marketing.

- A good all-purpose cleaner for last-minute showings, as well as plenty of paper towels.

- A separate phone number and answering machine to field calls, or an answering service.

If you have a cell phone plan with a low number of minutes, consider increasing your minutes so you can save yourself the hassle and money involved with installing a separate phone line. Using your cell phone for fielding inquiries about your home may be more beneficial because it allows you the flexibility to answer calls when you are not home. A call missed, even if it goes to voicemail and you return the call later in the day, may be a lost potential buyer. If you cannot answer calls during the day because you work, be sure to set up a specific voicemail message stating you will return the call within 24 hours.

Once you have these things in place, keep them handy and ready to use. Staying organized will help you stay calm and handle the process of marketing and selling the house with ease.

Additionally, you should know what homes in your neighborhood are for sale and when they are hosting open houses, as well as if the home is listed with a Realtor. Know the details of the house as well, including the size of the house, the number of bedrooms and bathrooms, and the house's condition. This will enable you to answer questions and comment on these homes compared to yours, as well as the general market.

When to Put Your House on the Market

Although houses come on the market throughout the year, spring is peak season for selling and buying a house. There are a number of reasons for this: In states that experience extreme winters, the spring allows buyers the first chance to house shop in nice weather, avoiding snow, ice, sleet, and rain. Secondly, this is the time buyers with children look for homes to avoid affecting their children's school year. Most parents would like to find a house in or around springtime, close, and move into the new home before the beginning of the next school year. This allows their children to finish the school year where they are currently attending and puts them in place to start a new school right at the beginning of the school year. The idea is that this will make the transition easier for the whole family.

According to U.S. News and World Report, most Americans move between May and September.

The downside of putting your home on the market during peak season is that the majority of people do, so there will be more homes to compete against. On the other hand, there are significantly more buyers looking for houses during this season. Although it does help to take advantage of the spring and summer house-buying season, there are buyers looking for new homes year round, and there are fewer houses for sale in the fall and winter, which trims down the number of homes for sale on the market. Overall, if spring works for you and your plans, then it is most beneficial to put your house on the market during this season, because you will be exposed to significantly more traffic and a higher demand.

Getting more specific, the best day of the week to put your home on the market is Saturday. If there are other homes in your area for sale holding an open house on Saturday, this will increase the chances that buyers going to the open house will drive by your home and see that it is newly listed for sale. It would be ideal to hold an open house the very first Sunday after you list the house, but even if this is not possible, you will still get significantly more exposure listing on a Saturday when there are open houses in your neighborhood.

Where to List Your Home

Today, it is estimated that more than 80 percent of people looking for a new home begin their search on the internet. The internet is your biggest ally in the FSBO process, as it will be the largest source of traffic and will give your home the most exposure to potential buyers. Within this medium, however, there are dozens of options and strategies to take.

The internet

There are many websites that exist specifically for listings of For Sale by Owner properties that offer a variety of options depending on what kind of exposure, help, and advertising you are seeking. All of these websites charge a fee, which ranges depending on service, to list and advertise your home on their website. Most of these websites offer national exposure and include listings across the country and also offer the option of listing your property on your local Multiple Listing Service (MLS) website.

The following are the most popular sites for FSBOs:

- **ForSalebyOwner.com (www.forsalebyowner.com)**: This site provides internet marketing services, real estate guidance and information, live customer support, downloadable legal forms, and a free database of homes to browse.

- **"FSBO" (www.fsbo.com):** Offers a flat-fee MLS generator, a home-search by state, a foreclosure search, FAQs, tips, real estate contracts, and much more.

- **HomesbyOwner.com (www.homesbyowner.com):** You can search for homes, find advertisement packages for your home if you are looking to sell, look into information on owning a FSBO business, and find networks of FSBO sellers.

- **Owners.com (www.owners.com):** On this site, you can look for home-selling tools, search home-buying resources, and find information on FSBO and buying a FSBO house.

- **ByOwner.com (www.byowner.com):** On this website, you can find rentals, land, FSBO houses, and resources if you are a FSBO seller, and find foreclosures.

- **Zillow.com (www.zillow.com/for-sale-by-owner):** This site allows you to post a listing for no charge with a video and unlimited pictures. Your home will be listed on Zillow as well as Trulia.

If you plan to list entirely on your own — which excludes using a discount brokerage — and do not want to expose your listing to Realtors because you do not want to pay a commission to them, then listing with one of these websites would be beneficial.

If you are selling a high-end home as a FSBO, consider advertising in higher-end outlets. After all, you want to attract the right buyer, and the right buyer may not be looking at FSBO websites. In certain regions, $500,000 would be considered very high-end, while in others, it is $1 million. If you are selling a high-end home, you will definitely need to expand the reach of your exposure and would do well to include some of the higher-end publications that cater to high-end homes such as the *Wall Street Journal* real estate section.

Websites on which to advertise higher end real estate include:

Luxury Real Estate (www.luxuryrealestate.com): This is one of the leading websites in the world dedicated specifically to luxury real estate listings around the world. To list, simply visit the website and click on the "Services" tab at the top of the page. Next, choose "Listing Properties With Us" and fill out the form requesting details of your house.

Premiere Properties Only (www.premierpropertiesonly.com): A specialized website for luxury and high-end FSBO listings. The website offers advertising and listing services for a flat fee per year, and can meet a variety of marketing and advertising needs. For instructions on how to list your property on the website, click "private sellers" from the company's home page.

International Listings (www.intlistings.com): A website specifically designed for high-end real estate listings from around the world. For $99, you can list your property, which will be exposed to more than 100,000 high-end buyers. The fee includes photo uploads, a property description, and your property's own website. The company will also e-mail you a report of how many times your listing has been viewed. To list on International Listings, simply click on "Add Your Listing Now" on the home page.

Services, Companies, and Professionals That Can Help

Because the process of selling a home can be complicated, and there may be specific areas of the process you are not comfortable with or good at, there is the option of hiring a professional to help you with specific areas of the home-selling process. You may want to hire a marketing expert, for instance, to create an Internet presence for you, a real estate attorney to guide you through the legal paperwork, or a real estate broker to expose your home to buyers.

What you can get out of these professionals and services depends on how much you want to invest in them. You can list your home with a flat-fee MLS service for a few hundred dollars; for a little more, you can hire a marketing expert or assistance service to create a market presence for your home and drive buyers to your listing. For a flat fee or commission of your sale price, you can give incentives to a buyer's agent to bring potential buyers to your home. It all depends on how much help you need and what your budget is.

CASE STUDY: BARRY WARDELL, ASSIST-2-SELL

Barry Wardell
www.assist2sell.com

In 1987, Assist-2-Sell founders Mary LeMeres Pomin and Lyle Martin left the traditional real estate industry and sought to meet a rising demand in the industry: high quality service for a reasonable price. Out of that demand came Assist-2-Sell, a full-service, flat-fee real estate company offering sellers the opportunity to save thousands while still obtaining the help many need to sell their home.

Before Assist-2-Sell, For Sale by Owner sellers in particular had few options when it came to enlisting professional help in the sale of a home. Most FSBO sellers choose to sell on their own because they are not willing to pay a high commission, typically 3 to 7 percent, to a real estate agent. After all, many agents spend significantly more time seeking future listings than they do marketing the homes they already have. "People would like to sell without paying exorbitant fees, but paying no fees is not always an option," said Barry Wardell, senior vice-president of franchise operations.

Assist-2-Sell uses a low-fee commission structure that enables sellers to choose services a la carte, which gives sellers the option to tailor their needs and pay for only the services they need. The company offers three general services to FSBO sellers. The first is the most basic: free marketing and advertising on the company's website, which benefits the company because sellers contact Assist-to-Sell directly, driving more traffic to their website.

The second option is a paperwork-only service, in which Assist-2-Sell guides a seller through the entire paperwork process and advises on complicated matters such as contract terms, inspections, and seller's disclosures. "The most nerve-racking part of the selling process is the paperwork," Wardell said. "Many sellers are unaware of the necessary paperwork they have to file." For instance, a seller may not know he has to file disclosures. Unless they know, they may not be aware they need this. FSBO sellers do not have contractual guidance, so they may not know they should include a timeframe for an inspection, for example, so they do not find themselves in the middle of an inspection five days before they are moving across the country.

With the paperwork-only service, "We tell them things such as who pays for what, we guide them through that, and help with inspections," he said. Although sellers can access boilerplate contracts and necessary forms from their state's real estate board or association website, contracts need to be tailored to fit each particular sale. When it comes to downloading forms and contracts "some states are not that user-friendly," Wardell said. With the paperwork-only service, sellers can rely on the professional guidance of an Assist-2-Sell broker to handle this part of the process and to ensure the seller has met all requirements and all the contracts are in the seller's best interest. With this service, Assist-to-Sell will also sit down with a seller and break down all the costs involved in the selling process, giving the seller a good idea of what he or she will be responsible for from the day the home is listed to the day the sale is closed.

The third service Assist-2-Sell offers is a flat fee listing service, the most expensive option. With most flat-fee MLS services and other discount brokerages, sellers' homes are automatically listed on the MLS site, whereas Assist-2-Sell offers clients the option to list on the MLS, or to just list on Assist-2-Sell's local website. A seller may not want to spend the money to list on an MLS site when they can spend much less and list on a local site. "The advantage is the buyer comes directly to Assist-to-Sell and there is no additional fee to list on MLS," Wardell said. If a Realtor brings in a buyer, either through the MLS service or directly through Assist-2-Sell's website, the seller will typically compensate the Realtor by paying him or her a flat fee or a percentage of the sale price. If a buyer comes directly to Assist-2-Sell without a Realtor, no commission is owed, just the flat fee. "It's all about providing more options," Wardell said.

One of the greatest challenges that FSBO sellers and buyers face is the lack of knowledge of the selling process. FSBO buyers and sellers typically do not know what to do next, which is the benefit to having a real estate agent to guide all parties through the entire process. "The agent's job is to keep the ball rolling," Wardell said. Without an agent's guidance, some FSBO sellers are unsure of what they need to do, such as schedule a meeting with a loan officer for instance, whereas an agent will make these appointments and keep everyone on track. Assist-2-Sell strives to provide this kind of structure and guidance without charging a 3 percent fee.

"For many FSBO sellers, the selling process is a mystery," Wardell said. "We try to take the mystery out of it, because it really is not a complex process. We are typically a seller's first call if they're struggling with legal requirements. We serve as the bridge; we become the catalyst when buyers don't know what to do next."

With more than 200 offices around the country, *Entrepreneur* magazine named Assist-2-Sell one of the fastest growing franchises, and it has saved sellers nearly a billion dollars combined since the company was founded. "Maybe we can help a family save money and put a kid through college or take a dream vacation," Wardell said. "Our fees help avoid short sales. Sometimes we may not be able to save people money, but perhaps we can save them some dignity."

As with anything, what you get is what you pay for when it comes to involving other parties and services in your FSBO sale. If you choose to pay a flat fee for an MLS listing, do not expect anything more than a listing. If you partner with a real estate agent and offer three percent for bringing you a buyer who purchases your home, you can expect that agent will work for you to bring in a buyer, because that agent wants his or her three percent.

So how do you know what option is best for you, and who you need to enlist to help you? First, take a step back and think about what you really need. Ask yourself:

Is my house located in a high-traffic area?

High-traffic areas include large cities as well as towns and other communities that draw many people. Houses on corners and near intersections are also in high-traffic areas. The more traffic your house is exposed to, the less help you will need in attracting buyers, which means listing on fewer websites and putting out fewer ads.

Is my house in a highly demanded area?

Established, older towns with good school systems and other attractive amenities are typically in higher demand than transient towns with bad school systems. If your house is in a highly demanded area, you may not need to offer a buyer's agent incentive to attract buyers; buyers will likely find you.

Am I willing and able to handle advertising and marketing on my own?

Creating a marketing strategy for your listing and then managing that strategy can be tedious and time consuming. If you are not good at managing detail and being persistent, consider hiring someone to handle the advertising and marketing for you.

Am I willing and able to access information needed to conduct an accurate CMA report?

If you are not comfortable completing a CMA on your own, or if you cannot access the information, then consider asking a Realtor to do it for you for free.

Realtor services

Some sellers prefer to remain 100 percent FSBO, and are not willing to pay a broker who brings in a buyer three percent. Other sellers are willing to pay a buyer's agent their percentage of the sale, or a flat fee, for their work to bring in a buyer. This option still saves you about three percent, the amount it would cost you to hire your own real estate agent to represent your home.

This option works best for people who are not in high-traffic areas, such as a neighborhood with a small population that is not near any major city or highway. In higher traffic areas, like any major city or popular suburban neighborhood, it may not be necessary to enlist the help of a Realtor. This option also works best for people who need to sell their homes quickly, or for people selling in a buyer's market. In a more challenging market for sellers, and in bad markets like Americans saw from 2007 to 2009, Realtors will also be more open to this option. When the market is good and Realtors have many listings, it is more challenging to find a Realtor who is willing to partner with FSBO sellers.

Although the typical fee for a buyer's agent is three percent, you can offer a Realtor a flat rate for bringing you a buyer, but be sure it is comparable to two or three percent of the sale of your home. After all, Realtors will still have the same amount of work to do representing a buyer of your property as they would otherwise, so you will not have much luck working with Realtors if you are not willing to properly compensate them for their services.

In order to find a Realtor, you will have to invest some time in the process. The way to initiate the process is to first send fliers to every real estate brokerage office in your area. Send them a flier with information about your property, details on what you are offering, and all of your contact information. You can also include the option of having the Realtor advertise your property through her firm. This can sometimes be beneficial for her if she do not have many good listings and would like to have a prime property to advertise.

Some Realtors will even run an open house for you as long as you agree to pay them an agreed-upon percentage should anyone coming to view the property and decide they want to make an offer. Some Realtors have buyers who are interested specifically in FSBOs, so tapping into this resource will optimize your exposure to these types of buyers, and others.

What to look out for

Whether or not you partner with a Realtor to market your house and bring in a buyer, you will likely get numerous calls from Realtors trying to get you to list your home with them. If you come across a Realtor trying to convince you to list with him, explain that you are not interested in listing with an agent, but inquire about his interest in taking a commission or flat fee for bringing you a buyer or advertising your home. You do not need to be working with just one Realtor to bring you a buyer, unless you decide to be exclusive with him and sign an agreement stating this. Otherwise, working with multiple agents to bring in buyers will increase your chances of finding a buyer.

While there are certainly thousands of reputable, professional, and ethical agents across the country, there are also those who will attempt to take the listing from you to get a commission. It is imperative to be knowledgeable and informed about the entire selling process and to ask many questions. This will help you avoid a similar situation, and will prevent unethical and unprofessional agents from unfairly benefiting from the sale of your home.

Even if you are working with a reputable agent you trust, be firm but polite with what you want, need, and expect from him. Some agents may feel they have more knowledge about the process than you. Many agents probably do, and will try to either steer you in another direction or take control of the process. You are your own advocate in the transaction, so be sure you are not backed into any corners.

Another factor to watch out for is Realtors who call stating they have a "potential buyer" when in fact they do not. Many do this to set up an appointment to preview the FSBO house for the supposed buyer, but their intentions are to get in the door to establish a relationship with you in hopes they can convince you to list the house with them. Not all Realtors will do this, but there are ones who may.

The best way to handle a call like this would be to ask the Realtor when he is able to bring the buyer to your home, otherwise you would prefer him take you off his call list. This will prevent the Realtor from setting up an appointment if he does not have a buyer, and simply trying to get you to list with them.

For Sale by Owner brokerages and MLS services

One of the most common services available to you as a FSBO seller through a For Sale by Owner brokerage is MLS, or Multiple Listing Service, a database used by Realtors that includes listings of homes around the country. There are a variety of companies that offer flat-fee MLS services, meaning you pay a flat fee for your home to be listed on the MLS website. Typically, these fees are around $500. On Flat Fee Listings, **www.flatfeelisting.com**, for example, you will pay a flat fee of $299 for your home to the listed on several MLS and local real estate websites. With discount brokerage Assist-2-Sell, sellers have the option whether they want to use the MLS service or if they want to list just with the company's listing service.

CASE STUDY:
"SELLING YOUR HOME DOESN'T
HAVE TO BREAK YOUR BUDGET"
John Henderson
FSBO turned Realtor
JT Henderson & Associates
www.simplymls.com

John Henderson began flipping houses in the early 1990s and has been in the real estate business ever since. He got his real estate license soon after he began flipping houses — buying a home and then re-selling it quickly in order to turn a profit — to comply with the laws in Michigan. "Due to the volume of homes I was flipping, I had to get my own real estate license. Because of that, I started helping others buy and sell property," Henderson said.

Over the following years, Henderson started his own business — JT Henderson & Associates — a real estate brokerage firm in Michigan that is one of the top ten in the state today. He founded the company in 2004 with the intention of creating a new concept in real estate, one that is centered on tailoring services to the needs of each client. "We offer full service as well as discount services. Clients, to reduce the cost of commissions, pay a flat fee of $499 to cover all the advertising costs of selling their home," Henderson said. "We offer flat fee to full service and anything in between. We can take over a transaction any time a home seller feels overwhelmed. Usually, a FSBO will want someone to take over during the negotiation stage."

The company charges a flat fee of $499 to any FSBO seller, which covers: all advertising, negotiations, and closing coordination. Together, the fees include: advertising on Michigan's local MLS website and the national MLS website, **www.realtor.com**; a comparative market analysis report and guidance from a JT Henderson agent on home pricing; an estimation of costs; negotiations with buyers; interior and exterior photos of your home; a yard sign and directional signs; access to a 24-hour telephone line; and a lock box system.

JT Henderson will also coordinate the closing for you and communicate with your title company. However, the company will not schedule showings or handle feedback from Realtors.

So how do sellers get all this for as little as $499? Essentially, a real estate agent provides four services: research, marketing, negotiating, and closing a transaction. Henderson's company provides these four services at a discounted price. Because sellers have to pay up to a 7 percent commission in a typical real estate transaction involving real estate agents, JT Henderson eliminates the 3.5 percent a seller would pay to an agent and charges just $499 to the seller. Clients must agree to pay a 3 percent commission to any agent who brings the client a buyer. If the sellers find a buyer on their own, the 3 percent commission is waived. JT Henderson & Associates charges 0.5 percent of the cost of the sale price of your home to cover the expenses and time involved in negotiating and coordinating closing on top of the $499 fee. If you use the company to purchase a new home, the 0.5 percent is waived.

"The best service I can provide FSBO buyers and sellers is good communication," Henderson said. "I always expect a sit-down with all parties involved to merge all of their discussions into a purchase agreement. Before that meeting, I have a telephone conversation with buyers and sellers individually to understand their expectations and educate them about the process. Most people only understand 40 percent or less of what is going to happen. Those phone conversations go a long way to help clarify the transaction."

When a seller finds a buyer, Henderson or an agent with his company serves as an intermediary. "As for requirements, before I get involved, I expect buyer and seller to come to agreement on at least two items: price and occupancy. If they haven't got that far, they really don't have a deal yet," Henderson said. "Once they've agreed to the most basic terms, it's time to bring in lenders, inspectors, and title company. While I do not demand they use the professionals I bring to them, I do expect them to consult with the people I trust to ensure the transaction is sound. Once we know we have a sound transaction, it's usually an easy step to handle the remaining details. This is when I sit down with all parties together to cover survey, inspections, deposits, and personal property," Henderson said.

According to Henderson, some of the biggest mistakes FSBO sellers make involve pricing. "Believing their home will sell for the same price as a house a Realtor is advertising down the block is a big misconception," said Henderson. "Most never research what the actual selling price is for homes in their in their area. Also, many FSBOs don't realize their transaction is regulated by state law. They will come to an agreement — often innocently — that is illegal. They become frustrated when agents, appraisers, or title closers will not close an agreement illegally," Henderson said. "Another issue is handling deposits. I've had to step in many times and threaten legal actions when parties do not comply with the terms of their purchase agreement."

Buyers are often most uncomfortable with handling the monetary aspects of the deal, Henderson said. "Handling earnest money deposits seems to be the most sticky issue with FSBOs." Once issues are ironed out, however, the process is fairly smooth. "Once we know we have a sound transaction, it's usually an easy step to handle the remaining details. This is when I sit down with all parties together to cover survey, inspections, deposits, and personal property. After the sit down, it's clear sailing through close."

Henderson and his staff of 20 agents have seen many successful FSBO sales since the company's founding in 2004 and have helped many people sell their home and save thousands. "I have found that most people just need a good education about the process and the laws involved."

The most commonly used MLS search engine is Realtor.com. This website will certainly expose your listing to thousands of potential buyers. When houses are entered into the MLS system, they are linked to the site's database, which you can only be listed on with an MLS listing. Keeping in mind that most buyers begin their house search on the Internet, so having your house listed on Realtor.com is crucial. One of the most affordable ways to get your home listed on MLS, and therefore on Realtor.com, is through a flat-fee MLS service.

With flat fee services, you will typically pay the fee up front and then you can create your listing. It is imperative to include a good description of your home, the asking price, and pictures, as well as your contact information. The information is entered into the MLS and you are listed as the contact person for interested buyers instead of a Realtor.

There are other professionals and companies that offer other services that do not include the MLS listing, but include things like marketing or handling paperwork. Usually, the fee for these services is a percentage of your sale price, or a flat fee.

These companies usually do not work with another Realtor, so you would not be obligated to pay an additional percentage to a Realtor. The problem with some of these services, however, is that many times the contract you sign with the company states that if your home does not sell within a certain period of time, say 60 days, the house is automatically listed on MLS. Then, the sale turns into a traditional 6 percent fee listing contract, so be sure to read the fine print before you sign any contract. Do not sign a contract that stipulates these terms.

With so many companies and services looking for your business and offering similar services, how do you know which ones are reputable? The best way to find a reputable company or online service is to get referrals from other FSBO sellers. You can ask people you know if they have sold FSBO, or try searching online at blogs or chat groups about FSBOs. For Sale by Owner Center, at **www.forsalebyownercenter.com**, is a great site for candid, first-hand information from FSBO sellers themselves.

Helpful Tip:

If you are considering using an assistance company like Help-U-Sell or Assist-2-Sell, ask for the company's sales record. You can also ask for referrals from previous clients; both will demonstrate their levels of success.

Assist-2-Sell and Help-U-Sell are two of the better-known companies offering FSBO sellers assistance. Help-U-Sell is a franchise, so your experience will greatly depend on what broker you work with at a certain location. Assist-2-Sell has offices across the country, and is a very reputable company.

Mortgage lenders

Mortgage lenders can be very helpful to you as a FSBO seller. It is important to research lenders and choose one to refer potential buyers to when they make an offer on your home. You will want to find a lender who is trustworthy — one you can rely on to qualify buyers for you. Finding a reputable lender will take some research, but should not prove extremely difficult. Mortgage lenders need exposure too, and they frequently work with for FSBO sellers in assisting with the marketing of the property, usually at no charge, in exchange for you referring potential buyers to them. It is not a bad idea to approach the lender who holds the mortgage on your home, if you have a mortgage, and offering her the option. After all, you have firsthand experience with the lender and already know she is trustworthy and reputable.

Lenders will sometimes assist you with fliers for your property, as they will want to include their own contact information on the flier along with yours. Make sure the lender is clear that she will put callers in touch with you if a buyer happens to call the lender first. Sometimes, lenders may ask to place a sign in your yard with their company information on it. Just be sure it is clear on the sign that callers should inquire with you first and not the lender.

Because buyers often visit a mortgage lender to get pre-qualified before they begin their house search, it can be beneficial to take some of your fliers to the lender and ask that the lender refer buyers to your home.

It is imperative to ask a lender you are considering working with if she is working with a Realtor, and if she is comfortable working with FSBO sellers. Just as there are unethical Realtors who will attempt to convince you to list with them, there are unethical lenders who may be working with a Realtor to refer FSBO listings to that Realtor. Be very clear in your listing that you do not wish to involve a Realtor.

Having assistance with your fliers and advertising can definitely save you some time and energy; just be clear about what you expect out of the lender. If, for instance, you would like the lender to replace and update fliers when the need arises, be sure to make this clear. If you would rather not include the lender's name and contact information on any of your advertising but would instead prefer to refer buyers to the lender when they make an offer, be clear about that as well. Do not assume anything, and as always, it is best to get all the details in writing.

Home inspectors

When a sale goes into contract, the buyer will typically hire a home inspector to do an inspection of the home. This is the point where your initial repairs and improvements will come in very handy, as home inspectors are trained to find problems with a home to alert the new buyers.

The buyer always chooses the home inspector. Never suggest one or choose one if the buyer asks you to; it should be their responsibility. This way, if a problem develops the buyer can only turn to the home inspector he or she chose, and cannot turn to you to blame for choosing the home inspector.

Home inspections are usually done within the first 15 days of the original contract date. This allows you a couple of weeks to complete the requested repairs and have the home inspected by the buyer themselves or the home inspector again to be sure the repairs were made.

Home inspectors are trained in school for a brief period of time to know a little about a lot. They know how to look for *indicators* of problems. For example, if your heating system has a problem, inspectors can detect there is in fact a problem, but will not necessarily be able to accurately identify the problem. In this sense, home inspections can be a bit of a headache for the seller because of the potential problems that arise from the inspection.

Since inspectors are not able to actually fix problems they identify, you will have to enlist the services of someone who can if a problem arises. For instance, a home inspector may identify a crack in the ceiling and advise that a structural engineer review the crack to determine its cause. Similarly, an inspector may detect mold in your laundry room, in which case you would have to hire a professional to remove the mold and clear the problem.

Inspectors are usually very cautious and will recommend that a structural engineer should review findings, but it by no means indicates that there is a structural problem with your home. In any event, the buyers will likely want an engineer to inspect any problems such as cracks in the ceiling.

If a home inspector suspects a problem, he should refer you to a specialist in that field for clarification on the problem; he should not make suggestions on the problem for most issues, but there are some exceptions. For example, if a window is leaking air between the panes and is clearly not cracked, it may be obvious to the inspector that the seal has broken and you need a new pane.

If he discovers a more significant problem, like a crack in the ceiling or a plumbing leak for instance, and advises you to hire a professional in that area to review the problem, be sure to do so. If a problem develops after closing, you have the receipt for the work and documentation that you hired an expert to fix the problem.

Home inspections and your contract

When you write a contract for the purchase of a house, the contract generally includes a dollar amount the buyer asks the seller to pay in required repairs needed, found by an appraiser or home inspector. On average, minimal repairs can be around $1,000 for an average-priced home in good condition. If the home has many problems, that amount can be much larger. Keep in mind this dollar amount must be agreed upon by both parties — you and the buyer — and you may wish to negotiate this.

For instance, if you agree to $1,000 in repairs and the home inspector finds $1,200 worth and the appraiser finds $800 worth of repairs, and all but one item on the appraiser's list for $150 is duplicated, then you have a total of $1,350 in repairs found. Because you only agreed to $1,000, you may choose to renegotiate the required repair amount. You can either agree to pay the additional fee or the buyer can agree to not have $350 worth of repairs done from the home inspector's list.

In addition to an inspector, a buyer may also hire an appraiser, as may be required by their lender, to appraise the home and identify any necessary repairs. The appraiser's recommended repairs will take precedence over home inspector required repairs because the lender will require all the repairs called for by an appraiser be complete prior to closing. Oftentimes, however, appraiser and home inspectors will find the same problems.

Appraisers

Many lenders require buyers to hire an appraiser to do an appraisal of a property they are interested in purchasing. The lender requires the appraisal to see if the house is worth the amount agreed to in the contract to purchase. The appraiser will look at the condition and selling price of comparable properties generally sold within one year of your contract date and within 1 mile of your home. It is quite common for the appraiser to come to the home and measure the inside and outside, take pictures, and check to see if everything is up to code. They will take all your home's features into consideration and determine a value for your home, which they will report back to the lender.

If a buyer has a government-insured loan, the appraiser will be check for the three S's: safe, sound, and secure. A government-insured loan requires a more thorough appraisal, and the FHA in particular requires a second appraisal for certain properties — those with a loan above $417,000, a loan to value ratio (the amount of the loan compared to the value of the property) of 95 percent or above, and houses found to be in a declining market.

Occasionally, a home will appraise for a different amount than the agreed contract price. Unless you find a factual error in the appraiser's report, you will likely either have to reduce the price to the appraised value, or move on to another buyer. The lender will only provide a loan for the amount the appraiser has appraised the home.

An example of this would be if your property sits on two lots totaling two acres and the appraiser noted that your property is only one acre. Check the appraiser's report for accuracy, particularly if their value is less than the purchase price.

Title companies and escrow agencies

A title company is responsible for conducting an "abstract of title," which is essentially an investigation into the history of the title to a house. The search determines who holds the title to the property and if the property has any liens or taxes due on it. Once the title company determines that the title is free of any liens, it will issue a Commitment of Title Insurance, which means the company will issue a title insurance policy.

Title insurance is an insurance policy that insures the buyer from any defects in the title, which can include liens and back taxes due on the property or claims of ownership from outside parties. This helps to guarantee that once you sell the property, your distant relative cannot claim to have any ownership rights to the property.

The title company actually handles the closing of the property. The lender will get all necessary information to the closing company. A closer, or point person assigned to handle the closing of your sale, is the person who works with the lender directly to accurately prepare the closing documents and will handle the closing process. They are trained for this somewhat tedious work, as it involves a lot of preparation, paperwork, and knowledge of legal details. They will also give you an overview of all the documents you will sign at the closing table.

Title companies can also be of assistance in giving you direction and help in writing the contract, where you can get forms, services, and so forth.

In some states, the buyer chooses the title company but it is not uncommon to discuss this with your buyer and agree on a company to use together. Usually the buyer's lender will have their own preferred closing company, which can be beneficial if the lender has a great relationship with the company and gives them a significant amount of business. The benefit is knowing that the company is reputable and capable of making sure the process and closing runs smoothly. The downside, although not all that common anymore, is if the closing company has a less-than-favorable reputation. If this is the case you will want to stand your ground and request that a different company be chosen by both you and the buyer and once you have decided, write it in the contract.

An escrow company is slightly different than a title company because an escrow company is primarily responsible for serving as a third party to hold and control funds for a real estate purchase. Escrow companies typically manage the transfer of money and do not have anything to do with the title or title insurance. Many title companies have an escrow division within their company that offers escrow services.

As the seller, a title company and an escrow company can be of great service to you by ensuring all your documents are in order and that the process is flowing smoothly. Because an escrow or title company will handle the closing, this is an added benefit to you, because you have a professional overseeing and managing the process.

Real estate attorneys

Though it is not too common for a buyer or seller engaging in a real estate transaction without the representation of a Realtor to hire a real estate attorney, it does on occasion become necessary. Real estate attorneys have a great deal of knowledge about contracts, seller's disclosures, the closing process, and other legal paperwork. They are also great at spotting and handling problems with the purchasing process, specifically with your contract.

**CASE STUDY:
FSBOS FROM AN
ATTORNEY'S PERSPECTIVE**

Robert Lattas
RE Law Chicago
www.relawchicago.com

Robert Lattas is a revered real estate attorney in Chicago who began his career at age 23. With a master's degree and a law degree under his belt, Lattas formed Lattas Law in 2001. Through his firm, he represents a variety of real estate transactions, and has extensive experience working with developers, corporations, and individual homebuyers and home-sellers. Lattas has grown quite a reputation for himself in the Chicago area as being an enthusiastic and knowledgeable attorney willing to work hard for the best interest of his clients, no matter who they are. In 2008, Lattas was featured in *Real Estate Executive*, Chicago's business and lifestyle magazine.

For the most part, Lattas works with Realtors he knows and trusts. They usually approach him to serve as the attorney at a closing for their clients because they are confident about Lattas' ability to handle the closing, get things done properly, and serve the best interest of their client.

Almost all of his FSBO clients have come from references, or people who have used him for a previous sale and want to sell on their own.

Over the years, Lattas has handled many FSBO transactions and in his experience, handling FSBOs is more challenging from an attorney's standpoint. This is simply because of the additional work involved that usually falls to the attorney. "The experience is different in FSBO," Lattas said. "It's a lot more difficult because a seller wants to do the deal themselves and a buyer goes into it thinking it's a good deal. Most of the time, it is a good deal, but it's the "stuff" that happens in between that gets complicated.

That "stuff" includes obtaining transfer tax stamps, hiring an inspector, dealing with an appraiser, doing a final walk-through, drawing up contracts, marketing, determining a price, and so on. "It is a lot more work for attorneys handling FSBOs because we have to advise them on a lot of issues," Lattas said. Attorneys are not familiar with many of these areas, such as marketing. "We need to do things like advise them when to be home and what to fix for the inspection," he said. If there is no Realtor, Lattas Law has to create the contract, and often FSBO sellers are not aware of what they should include in it.

One of the biggest mistakes FSBO sellers make, according to Lattas, is using a standard contract that is not specific to the particular state in which the sale is occurring. Each state has different local laws, contingencies, and customs that will affect a real estate sale. The standard Realtor fee, for instance, varies from state to state as do inspection requirements. While using a boilerplate contract is perfectly fine as a starting point, a contract should include clauses and conditions that speak to the specifications of each sale.

The other significant mistake Lattas sees FSBO sellers make is pricing their home too high, a common mistake. "You have to know what your home is worth," Lattas said. It means nothing what you paid for it." Sellers can determine an appropriate selling price by listening to the demands of the market, and by comparing similar properties in their neighborhood. Additionally, FSBO sellers should be cautious about some companies and services that offer free services. Some of these companies charge you nothing, but they also give you nothing.

In Lattas' experience, FSBO is the last option for some people facing a short sale or a foreclosure. When a seller is losing money on a property already, the last thing they want to do it to have to pay a 7 percent commission. Lattas also noticed home sellers become more innovative during the housing market crash that began in 2008 to provide buying incentive. "Sellers have become more creative, providing closing costs, leaving items them would normally take like flat screen TVs," said Lattas. "I've even seen sellers give away Chicago Bears tickets!"

Despite the fact that a FSBO transaction can mean significant more work for an attorney without necessarily more money, selling FSBO can be very beneficial if a buyer knows what he is doing. "Especially if you're in a high traffic area, such as on the corner of a busy neighborhood, it eliminates what the Realtor® does," he explained, and makes it much easier for a seller to draw traffic to their home, and ultimately, be a successful FSBO seller.

If you are not familiar with the legal requirements and paperwork involved in a home sale, it is wise to hire an attorney to oversee just this part of the process.

Chapter 7

Staging Your Home

ow that you have organized, made repairs, cleaned, listed your home, and possibly planned an open house, it is time to stage your home for potential buyers. Staging, by definition, involves making changes to accentuate the positive features of your home and downplay what are the perceived negatives of your house. These changes can range from the color of walls to the placement of furniture.

Staging is necessary especially during a buyer's market, when competition is high among sellers. It can be an integral part of the strategy to get your house sold as quickly as possible. Staging can give your home that extra sparkle it needs to set it apart from the others and attract the right buyer. Fortunately, you do not need to purchase much to stage your home. Particularly if you are creative, it is very easy to work with what you already have. It is, however, important to de-clutter your home before you stage it.

There are a variety of furniture rental companies to rent furniture for staging your home. At Brook Furniture Rental, **www.bfr.com**, you can choose from a variety of options to custom create a look for each room in your house. Check the website for available delivery areas — they do not deliver to all areas of the country. AFR Furniture Rental, at **www.rentfurniture.com**, and Cort, at **www.cort.com**, are other companies that offer furniture rental for staging purposes.

Most buyers are looking for a house that is current and trendy, not outdated in style and design. If the decorating style in your house is more than 10 years old, then it may be considered outdated. If you feel you do not have the appropriate furniture to effectively stage your home, rent furniture for staging purposes. This is a significant investment, but may mean the difference between a sale and your home sitting on the market for six months.

Staging is by no means a tool to hide anything negative about your home, but a tool to maximize your home's potential and put that on display for buyers. You should expect to invest at least some money in staging your home. Typically, hiring a stager to give you an initial consultation costs about $300 and goes up from there depending on how much work is involved. If you have to rent furniture, it can cost significantly more and depends on what kind of furniture you choose and where you are located.

Even if you use your own furniture and do not have to rent any big pieces, accessories like fresh flowers and small furniture pieces can make a big difference and add to the positive feel of your home.

If you are not the creative type or if you need some ideas for staging your home, conduct some research. Magazines like *Better Homes and Gardens* and *Martha Stewart Living* are great resources for ideas on staging. You can also scour catalogs from home furniture or home improvement stores for ideas. Another great option is to browse through the Home décor feed on Pinterest, an inspirational image-sharing social media network (**www.pinterest.com/categories/home_decor**). The goal is to get a specific style or design in mind that you feel fits your home and that is possible with the furniture you have already.

Room to Room Staging Tips

Staging enables you to highlight each room's strengths, like size and natural light. It also helps to highlight special features, such as a fireplace. Knowing how to optimize each space in your house will enable you to create a clean, balanced look for your entire house that connects each room to the other.

The living room

When you stage your living room, you want to optimize traffic flow in the room. You also want to make the most of the sight lines. A sight line is the view you have of a room. When buyers enter the living room, you want them to get the best view of every good feature, including the room's size and style. Any focal points of the room, like a fireplace, need to be highlighted. Arranging furniture around the fireplace will help accentuate it, for instance, and will draw attention immediately to the fireplace when buyers walk into the room.

To further accomplish this, arrange the furniture in a way that buyers can get a clear view of everything in the room with little to no distractions. Typically, furniture is clustered together in an effort to create cozy seating areas. However, when showing your house, you want it to be less about function and more about maneuverability.

To make the best use of floor space and create optimal traffic flow, remove all baskets and magazine racks on the floor. With these, you should also remove all decorative elements such as statues, books, small plants, and things of that nature. Doing this allows buyers to see the full extent of the space. Keeping your large area rugs is fine, but remove the small ones, as they tend to be a distraction and break up the flow of the space.

Make the living room bright with at least three lamps in addition to any overhead lighting. You may have two table lamps and a floor lamp arranged triangularly, but you should break these up and distribute them in different areas of the room. They should be dispersed to spread the light evenly across the room. The lampshades should be white or off-white in color, allowing light to shine through easily. Dark lampshades hide the light and prevent it from illuminating and enhancing the selling features. You also want to be careful not to block natural light. This may require you to remove window treatments or blinds, especially if you have plastic blinds that are dirty, yellowed, and outdated. Pull back any drapes as far as possible to allow the natural sunlight to light the room.

If you have bookcases, remove 50 to 60 percent of the books and any other trinkets or items so the bookcase is only half full. Keep older, classy, hardcover books that add elegance to the room and organize these neatly and evenly throughout the space.

If you have a fireplace, be sure to clean it out thoroughly and polish any fire tools, screens, and accessories you have next to the fireplace. You want to keep the mantle de-cluttered, with only one or two items, like a picture, candles, or vase. A mirror can help reflect light into the room as well as create an open feeling.

The item of décor you choose to hang on each wall needs to be neutral in style and not taste-specific. Landscapes and still-life paintings work well to add color but do not attract a great deal of attention. On your coffee table, which should be near the center of the room, create a unique centerpiece that will draw attention, like a candle and flower arrangement.

Spice up your solid-colored sofa by accenting it with a few pillows with a texture or a pattern. Do the same for your sitting chairs and loveseats. If your sofa is already patterned with a colorful print, like a floral design, consider purchasing a modern sofa cover that is a solid color. If you cannot purchase a new sofa, consider buying a slipcover in a sold, neutral color to fit over your existing sofa. You can find inexpensive sofa slipcovers at Overstock (**www.overstock.com**), Smart Bargains (**www.smart bargains.com**), Get Slip Covers (**www.getslipcovers.com**), or discount retailers.

The kitchen

The kitchen can make or break a deal. The condition and appearance of the kitchen is an important issue and weighs heavily in a purchase decision. The kitchen is fairly easy to stage because there is not too much furniture to move around. The most important thing in your kitchen is the countertops — if they are in poor condition, consider painting them. Select the right primer and a neutral color. If they are extremely dated and ruin the look of the kitchen (and painting will not help), then you should consider replacing them with corian or granite.

If you have blinds, curtains, shades, or anything on your windows, remove them to optimize the natural light. Natural light will also make your kitchen look bigger. When you remove window treatments, be sure to thoroughly clean your windows, both inside and out. If your kitchen has an island, clear everything off with the exception of one or two focal point items, such as a bowl of fresh fruit or a small vase of flowers. It is a good idea to discard or at least put away your hand towels and get new ones. This can bring color into your kitchen, but avoid floral patterns and bold colors, and instead choose solid, neutral colors.

Be sure you have cleared out all of your personal items, like baskets of keys and mail, and any knickknacks. Leave minimal items out on the countertops for display. The more you have on your counters, the smaller the space will look. If you have a hanging pot rack or hanging utensils in the kitchen, take them down. These distract from the size and flow of the kitchen. Find a space for your trashcan either under the sink or in a cabinet. Take down all your pictures, magnets, and other items from your refrigerator and wipe down the surface to remove any fingerprints or stains.

The master bedroom

Next to the kitchen and bathrooms, the master bedroom is one of the most important rooms in your home when it comes to attracting buyers. The master bedroom should convey relaxation and tranquility, and again, be as neutral in color and tone as possible. Buyers often look to fulfill a dream and a certain lifestyle when purchasing a house, and this room should reflect that idea.

A queen-size bed is ideal for the master bedroom, although a king-size bed will work if the room is large enough. When decorating your bed, be sure to use only neutral-colored bedding and accent with color by using a throw blanket and one or two matching pillows. If you have a comforter with a pattern or loud print, consider removing it and purchasing an inexpensive white or cream-colored blanket to cover your bed instead. Use light-colored sheets and pillowcases to match the color tone of the bed.

On your dresser, leave only one decorative or accent piece on the dresser and/or chest of drawers and focus it in the center of the surface. The accent piece can be a jewelry box, candle arrangement, or a mirrored tray with a few trinkets.

As for your walls, remove any photos that clutter the walls and hang one picture on one or two walls that is proportionate in size and not distracting, but rather complementing, to the room. If you have accent rugs in your bedroom, remove them to make the room look larger and maintain the flow of the room. It is best to have less furniture. If you can store extra pieces of furniture, especially if it is dark that makes a room look smaller, do so.

The extra bedrooms

The focal point of the bedrooms should always be the bed. The bed should be easily visible from the doorway and be the dominant fixture in the room, especially with extra bedrooms that are smaller than a master bedroom. The extra bedrooms should demonstrate flexibility to the buyer, as they may be used for a children's room, a nursery, an office, or a media room. The buyer should be able to envision his or her own purpose for the room when he or she walks into the room.

Extra bedrooms should be as gender neutral as possible. This opens up the possible use of the bedrooms to the imagination of the buyer. You do not want themes that specifically designate the room as gender-specific, especially themes painted on the walls or wallpaper borders. If your extra bedrooms serve as your children's rooms and are not neutral in color, consider taking down any wallpaper and painting over walls with a soft, neutral color. Similar to the master bedroom, beds in extra bedrooms should be simply decorated with a neutral-colored quilt, perhaps a complementing throw, and a few throw pillows.

As you did in the living room, remove all baskets, magazine racks, and small plants, and place a lamp on either side of the bed. These can be either a stand-alone or a table lamp if you have nightstands at the sides of the bed. Be sure to keep your décor and accent pieces to a minimum and neutral in color and style. Place only one decorative item on the dresser and chest of drawers. Keep nightstands clear of trinkets and clutter. Only a lamp or alarm clock should be on nightstands.

The dining room

When buyers walk through a dining room, they want to be able to picture their own family get-togethers and holidays. You want the room to be warm and inviting. The best way to do this is with soft lighting. Consider replacing the bulbs in your lamps and chandelier with a low-watt bulb (40 watts or less), which will evoke a softer feeling.

If your dining room is presently used for something other than dining, such as a workout room or play area for children, convert it back to a dining room for the process of selling the house. Like the other rooms in your home, you should only have a few pieces of furniture in the room to make it feel as spacious as possible. Limit the furniture in this room to a dining room table and chairs, a chandelier or light fixture, and one other piece, such as a china cabinet.

The dining room table should be in the center of the room, the focal point, centered underneath a chandelier or light fixture. Most homes have a light fixture hanging from the ceiling, indicating where the center of the table should be. Make your dining room table as small as possible by removing the leaves — this creates more room. Leaves are extended parts of the table that can be folded down on the ends. The ideal number of chairs at the table is four. Have no more than six, as this will cramp the space and take away from the room. People should be able to walk around the table with ease.

Assuming your dining room table is in good condition, use a table runner or placemats to accentuate the wood. Do not use both, and avoid tablecloths. Add a nice centerpiece, like a bouquet of fresh flowers or a candle arrangement. Remove everything from the table besides your runner or place mats and your centerpiece. You should not have items such as salt and pepper shakers or other condiments at the center of your table.

On the walls in your dining room, remove any pictures or art work that clutter the room. Artwork should be generic in style, and removed if it is not. Using a nice large mirror on the walls can really help the room look bigger. If you have a liquor cabinet in your dining room, be sure all the liquor out of sight, as this may be offensive to some buyers.

Like in the living room, take advantage of any natural light from windows by pulling back drapes or curtains to let as much natural light in as possible. If you have any area rugs in your dining room, make sure it centered underneath the table, which should be centered under the chandelier. An area rug can really add character and dimension to the room but be sure the size of the rug is proportionate to the room and the dining table and chairs.

Finally, there should be no more than three items on each side of the wall, with the tallest piece in the center and the two smaller pieces tucked next to the taller piece on either side. If you have one large piece of furniture like a china cabinet, center it on one of the walls opposite the dining room table to balance the feel of the room.

The bathrooms

Bathrooms are one of the least costly rooms to stage once you have completed the de-cluttering process, made repairs, and cleaned. Your goal with the bathroom is to create a spa-like atmosphere. Since you cannot rearrange your bathroom, make it appear spacious with bright lighting.

Bathrooms can also be the most difficult to stage because most things are difficult to change, like the floor, bathtub, and sink fixtures — unless you invest the time and money to do so. If you have a color in your bathroom that is hard to work with, like brown and yellow tiles on your floor, do not emphasize this by adding accent pieces that have the same color.

Bring more white and cream to the room to distract from any unattractive features, like an outdated floor. If you have an outdated floor with dark colors, like brown, purchase a large white or cream bathroom rug to brighten the bathroom. Replace your shower curtain with a white or cream-colored curtain and keep it closed for open houses and showings. Remove everything from the shower or bathtub. If you have a window in your shower, remove the blinds or curtains and keep the window bare to allow as much natural light in as possible.

To match the neutral-colored rug and shower curtain, use new towels in the same color and arrange them neatly on the towel rack. Pick one matching hand towel to contrast your shower curtain. Accessorize with one or two thick candles, decorative guest soaps, and a simple soap dispenser.

Entrances and exits

Your entrances and exits should be as functional and clutter-free as possible. The most important entrance is the foyer, the first space you see when you walk in the home. These spaces can easily be overwhelmed with shelves, knickknacks, and pictures. Purchase a new mat to place at the foot of the front door to welcome potential buyers. If you do not have any plants or shrubbery framing your door, consider purchasing small plant holders for each side of the door. Depending on how big your stoop is, use small plants or trees in the plant holders to frame your door, but be sure not to overwhelm the space. You simply want to add a small touch to your front door, not hide it.

Your foyer needs to speak to the excellence of the house. The look and feel should be the same as when you walk into a nice hotel's lobby. To do this, keep your colors neutral and complementary of the entire house. A thin side table will add a focal point and demonstrate the functionality of the space. If you have the room, place a small lamp on the side of the table or on the table. If there is room for seating, a bench or chair can add a nice touch to this room.

If you do not have a large foyer but only enough space for perhaps a picture and small area rug, use your most attractive piece of art and coordinate the colors in the piece with the rug and the color of the walls, if possible.

Lighting is just as important in your entrance rooms as the other rooms in your home, so replace broken bulbs with new ones. Remove colorful or decorated light switch covers and replace with white or off white. As for some of the other entrances in your house, be sure there are no nameplates, posters, or "Keep Out" signs on any of the doors leading to bedrooms off the hallway.

Stairways and hallways need similar attention. Keep these areas clutter-free and limit the amount of pictures and other items hanging on the walls. To add brightness and depth to these areas, hang mirror at the end of a hallway to make the space look bigger. Another decorative piece that is neutral yet attractive is a wall clock. Add color and warmth to an entryway or hallway by placing a rug or runner down the length of the hallway.

The home office

If you have a home office, it is best if you have only a desk, office chair, and perhaps a bookshelf in the room. Most offices are a small room compared to the rest of the rooms in the house, so limiting the furniture in this room will eliminate an overcrowded feeling.

As with other rooms, the lighting in the office needs to be bright. Make sure to optimize natural light by pulling back drapes or curtains and pulling up or removing blinds. Your desk should be placed in the center of the room, in such a way that it faces the door to the room.

Organize your files and equipment so that it is still functional for you while you are showing your home. You do not want to make so many changes that your office is not functional while your house is on the market, but you do want to tidy up the space and stage it properly. Remove all but a few photos and framed awards from the walls, and remove and store any electronic equipment you can do without. Tuck cords and wires neatly out of sight.

If you have a bookcase, remove about half of the books and store them away. This helps to open up the room and keep it from looking cluttered. After all, you want to give the impression your office is organized and enhances productivity.

Always be sure to turn your computer off when showing the house so as to not reveal anything personal that you may be working on. Do the same with any personal information you may have.

The basement

If you are like most people you use your basement to store large items like suitcases, air conditioners, unused furniture, and everything else you want out of sight. While buyers do understand that a basement is a storage area, it is best to create what you can out of the space.

If you have furniture in the basement, stage it as you staged your living room with the furniture centered in a seating area. Remove any boxes, extra furniture, and any other miscellaneous items from the main room in your basement and neatly stack boxes in a separate closet if you have one. It is best to remove any extra furniture to storage to optimize the space in the basement.

As with any other room, you want to keep the basement de-cluttered and clean to optimize the space. Check that all the lights work in the basement and that all the closets or storage areas, including the boiler room, are free of clutter. Remove any curtains you have on the windows and clean the windows to allow in the natural light. This is especially important in the basement because of the minimal amount of windows and natural light in most basements.

In addition to these basic rooms, you may have a library, study, sunroom, music room, or sewing room that will also need staging. If you stick with the sleek, simple, and clean theme, staying current in style and design like you have done for the rest of your home, you will find staging these rooms easy.

Creating Curb Appeal

Buyers tend to make snap judgments about your house based on their first impression, which is why the outside of your home should be well kept, maintained, and inviting. To get a good idea of your home's curb appeal, go outside, stand across the street from your house, and get a buyer's view of the property. Ask your neighbors for their honest opinion of your home.

If your house lacks curb appeal, you risk that the buyer will scroll right past your listing on the internet or drive by without stopping to get more information. Fortunately, there are some simple and inexpensive ways to create curb appeal if your home needs some help. One of the first things to consider is whether the house or the trim needs to be painted. If cleaning and power washing were not enough and you think you need paint, this can add tremendously to the curb appeal of your home. As usual, stay away from bold colors on the exterior and go with white, light grey, soft beige, or tan to brighten up the outside. Take a look at the other homes on your block and try to tailor the style of yours to the overall look of the neighborhood. If you do not want to paint the entire house, consider painting just the trim, shutters, down spouts, and gutters. Painting the house or just the accent features makes for a big return on the investment so it is well worth it.

If you feel the outside of your home is lacking something, consider getting shutters, which come in a variety and styles and can give your house a competitive edge, especially if you live in a neighborhood where all the houses are similar in style and design.

The lawn

A freshly mowed lawn helps to give buyers the impression that the house is well maintained. Fertilize your grass to help give it a lush, green, healthy look, which is especially important in the spring and summer. When you mow, be sure to bag the grass clippings.

It is also important that you weed and edge your lawn to give it that perfectly manicured touch. Mowing without edging and weeding is like having great makeup and messy hair. It just does not look nearly as good.

Shrubbery and flower beds

Remove any dead or dying trees, shrubs, or hedges and replace them if necessary to maintain the look of your landscaping. Prune anything overgrown or dying and cut back anything that blocks windows and keeps light from entering the house. Also make sure there are no weeds or grass in the flowerbeds.

Adding seasonal flowers in your flowerbeds is an inexpensive way to add color and charm to your home. Place little flowers toward the front, and larger flowers, shrubs, and bushes toward the back. Keep the flowers watered and weeded during the entire time your home is on the market, all the way to closing. In fact, it is important that you continue to care for and maintain the entire house until you close.

Replace old mulch around trees, flowers, and in flowerbeds. You would be surprised how much new mulch can liven up your landscaping. Consider adding a border around your landscaping, such as a line of bricks, rocks, or concrete that frames your landscaping. This will give your yard a clean-cut look.

Keep in mind that if you do not have the time or equipment to landscape on your own, hire someone to do it. If you already work with a gardener or landscaper, explain your new vision to them. The return on investment for landscaping is fantastic, and it is not very expensive to keep the lawn and landscaping maintained.

Sidewalks and driveways

After power washing your sidewalks and driveways, keep them swept and free of debris and leaves in the spring, summer, and fall and free of ice and snow in the winter while the house is up for sale.

Windows

Windows are a very important aspect of a home. If you have older windows and the wood window frames are peeling or cracking on the outside, consider painting the trim with a bright white color. Be sure to keep your windows clean inside and out throughout the marketing period.

The most important thing to remember when staging is less is more. If you cannot afford to rent new furniture and store your current furniture, there are many options to use what you have on a budget. As long as you are willing to take the time to review what needs to be done to your home to optimize its appeal, you will be in a great position to attract that perfect buyer who falls in love with your home.

Chapter 8

Marketing Your Home

Marketing is a very important part of selling your home. Without proper marketing, all your cleaning, de-cluttering, and improving will mean nothing when you cannot sell your house.

There are a variety of advertising options that include the use of signs, newspapers, bulletin boards, MLS sites, fliers, and blogs. Like with listing your house, consider what you need before you devise a marketing strategy. If your house in a high-traffic area, like on a corner or busy intersection, or if your house is located in a highly demanded area or in a busy city, you may not need as much advertising as a house in a rural area.

Signs

The easiest way to market your house and let buyers know it is for sale is by placing a "For Sale by Owner" sign in your front yard. You can purchase these signs at most large home improvement stores. These stores generally carry two or three styles to choose from, a basic black and white on plastic, a red and white on plastic, and then also those same color options on metal. The red and white metal is usually the best choice as they are brighter and sturdier in bad weather. You can also create a custom, two-color sign from a sign shop for reasonable prices.

On the sign, include the following information:

- Contact phone number with area code
- The number of bedrooms in your home
- The number of bathrooms in your home
- The size of your garage
- The square footage of the house, if the house is large. If the house is small, under about 1,500 square feet, leave this information off the sign.

You may wonder why you want to bother with anything more than the phone number if you are going to have a box with fliers.

You will do this if you happen to run out of fliers or if someone is driving by and does not stop for a flier. This little bit of information simply gives the lookers a snapshot of the house so they can determine if it meets their basic needs.

Example of a For Sale by Owner Sign:

For Sale by Owner
3/2/2
919-555-1212

The "3" in the numerical sequence represents the number of bedrooms, the first "2" represents the number of bathrooms, and the last "2" represents how many cars the garage will hold.

To have an effective sign, you need more than just one in front of your home. You should also have arrow signs strategically placed to direct traffic into your neighborhood and to your home. To do this, purchase a few "home for sale" arrow signs at the same place you get the main yard sign. You will want one placed at the entrance to your neighborhood, perhaps an area where traffic merges to the main street of your town. Place the sign where it is visible to traffic traveling in both directions.

To draw more attention to signs, especially signs advertising open houses, tie balloons to the sign. However, leave the balloons on the sign for only a day or two and then remove them for about a week. For the next open house, use different colored balloons.

It is important to keep the same people's attention, like your neighbors and other people who live in your extended community. This way, you can optimize your word of mouth advertising. If someone in your neighborhood knows anyone, perhaps a family member, friend, or co-worker who is looking for a home in that community, that person will have your listing in mind.

Beyond placing a "House For Sale" sign at the entrance into your neighborhood, use directional or arrow signs at intersections to lead traffic through your neighborhood and to your home. If you live in the back end of your neighborhood and there are several turns to reach your home, strategically place arrow signs from the main road to your street. You do not need to put your contact information or details of your home on the signs you place at entrances into your neighborhood or at intersections. Your goal with these signs is to simply drive traffic to your home, where the details will be visible on your yard sign.

Place signs at intersections of main roads that are near your home, even if the intersection is in a neighboring community. This will draw traffic from beyond your neighborhood.

Advertisements

In addition to signs, you definitely want to list your house in your local newspaper's classified section. There is really no need for anything more than a one-line ad. Place an ad on every bulletin board you come across in all of your local grocery stores and restaurants — these are great places to put up fliers. You should also list it for sale in any free community or church bulletins you can find. There are a variety of places to place an ad for free, and it can be very beneficial to your marketing.

What style is your house?

Colonial: Colonials are houses built to resemble homes from the colonial period (about 1600 to the mid-1800s). Typical style is traditional, square-shaped with two stories and five windows on the second story of the home on front of the house and four windows on the first floor with a door in the center of the windows.

Ranch: Ranches are low to the ground, often one to one-and-one-half story, or split-level, and L-shaped with large picture windows.

Cape (or Cape Cod): Capes are usually low like a ranch, made of wood, and covered with shingles. They are usually smaller, with one to one-and-one-half floors and a few small windows on either side of a centered door on the front of the house.

Farmhouse: Farmhouses are usually large, open-space homes with wraparound porches, multiple fireplaces, and multiple windows lining the first and second stories of the home.

Tudor: The Tudor is a Renaissance-style defined by archways, asymmetrical design, stonework, steeply pitched roofs, and large bay windows. The usually have multiple stories, with entrances on the sides of the house instead of in the front.

Bungalow: A bungalow is typically a small one-story, cottage-type house with a low roof, a large porch, and a large attic.

Cottage: Similar to the Tudor in style, with low-arched doorways, brick or stone siding, and several stories. There are a variety of cottage styles that differ depending on style.

Victorian: Victorian houses are very tall and narrow and resemble a gothic style with several stories, steep roofs, wraparound porches, narrow colored glass windows, and detailed molding.

One very important aspect people tend to overlook is advertising your home outside of your own community. If you live in a metropolitan area, advertise in the entire area. Place fliers in grocery stores and restaurants that are within a 30-minute drive of your community. Ask if you can place fliers at all factories and large employers in your area as well as military bases. If these employers put out a newsletter of some kind, ask if you can place a small ad in their business. This can be free or very inexpensive.

Abbreviations to describe your home are ideal to use in advertisements to optimize your space while minimizing your words. Some common abbreviations to use in an ad include:

a/g pl: above ground pool	fm or fr: family room
a/c: air conditioner	fp: fireplace
apt: apartment	f-bmt: finished basement
ba: bath	gar: garage
balc: balcony	lrg: large
bd or br: bedroom	liv or rm: living room
bkyd: backyard	mk: modern kitchen
bsmt: basement	ofc: office or study
bung: bungalow	pat: patio
d/w: dishwasher	pl: swimming pool
w/d: washer/dryer	sq ft: square feet
eik: eat in kitchen	txs: taxes
fdr: formal dining room	wlkin: walk in closet
ffbr: first floor bedroom	yd: yard

It also may be beneficial to run a small line ad in the classified section of large cities in your region of the country. For example, if you live in Oklahoma City, advertise in Tulsa, Oklahoma, and Dallas, Texas as well. There is a lot of traveling between these two cities and Oklahoma City. Although this can be a fruitful advertising method, it can be slightly expensive and may not be entirely necessary, especially if you live in a high-traffic area already.

Effective versus ineffective ads

When you write an ad for a newspaper, keep it short, specific, and to-the-point, and use effective adjectives to describe your house that will draw buyers. Keeping the ad short will not only accommodate the limited space of a newspaper, but it will also keep a buyer's attention long enough to read the entire ad — which should take only a few seconds. An ad can be as short as one line, but should not be any longer than four to five lines depending on how much information you need to include without including more information than is necessary.

What exactly is necessary to include in an ad? Typically, the following is included:

- Number of bathrooms
- Number of bedrooms
- Price
- Contact phone number (do not include an address)
- Special features like a pool, central air conditioning, or fireplace
- Website, if there is one

Include the phrase "By Owner" or "FSBO" to let the buyer know you are selling on your own and when they call the contact number, he will be calling you directly. Beyond that, using one short phrase to describe your house is a good idea. The goal is to use a phrase that appeals to the emotions.

Be creative and use softer words, such as "spacious," and "relaxed" in place of the typical adjectives like "big," or "large." Your ad should evoke a feeling about your house, and create an incentive for a buyer to come see it. In addition to the basic information, consider including a phrase that highlights your home's best feature, such as:

- "An Outdoor Lover's Dream," for a large backyard or a house in the country
- "Cook Out in Style," for a backyard with a barbecue
- "Country Cozy in the City," for a small apartment or house in the city
- "This Home Has it All," for a house with many special features

If the best feature about the house is its location, include a phrase like:

- Ideally located
- Prime location
- Desirable location
- Close to everything

Effective ads are short and specific in describing a house. For instance:

Cozy 2+1 with views of the city
secluded, f/p, a/c, parking, a must see
$229K, By Owner, 555-1212

Fliers

While you are purchasing your signs, purchase a flier box as well. If you cannot find one at the home improvement store, you will likely be able to find one at a sign shop, as these stores usually keep them in stock for Realtors. Place this flier box between your sign and the road. Put it fairly close to the road so the potential buyers wanting a flier will not have to walk far into your yard and ideally would not even have to get out of the car.

When it comes to your fliers, you can get a map of the city and place stickers where you have concentrated your advertising and then create a list of the places you put fliers and advertised in so it is easy to refer to and keep up with.

The goal with a flier is to provide enough information to educate buyers to the wonderful features of the home, but not so much they feel they do not have to look at the house at all. The flier should include a catchy paragraph highlighting the features of your home, all of the basic information, and your contact information. Make sure the flier is neat and readable.

In general, you do not want to include pictures of the inside of the house on the flier. Often, a picture on a flier simply will not do a room justice and many times will make it look much darker or smaller than it really is. If you have one or two great pictures of the interior that appropriately depict a room in your home, consider including it. Otherwise, you need only to use an outside picture of your home for the flier because a buyer may be looking at homes for sale, gathering fliers and information, and by the time they get home and sift through the fliers, they may not be able to recall which one was which and the ones they really liked just based on the address. The picture will help them place your home.

Pick the best feature of your home that captures the feel and create a headline for your flier, like the one you used in your advertisement. Include your headline at the top of your flier. Under the headline, place the exterior picture of the house. Below that, insert a paragraph that may read something like this:

This gorgeous home has everything your family
needs to grow and live in comfort and style.
From the bright, spacious and well-designed kitchen

> to the spa-like master bathroom with jetted tub
> and double vanity!
> For a private viewing, call
> Jane Doe
> 555-555-1212
> Or e-mail buymyhousenow@yourwebsite.com

Next, list the features of your home, including:

- The number of bedrooms
- The number of bathrooms
- The size of the garage
- Any additional rooms your home has, like a study or an office

Then go on to specific features your house may have versus other homes, such as:

- Large island or eat-in kitchen
- Fireplace
- Two living rooms
- Bonus room upstairs
- Storage shed
- Sprinkler system
- Swimming pool
- Central air

Feel free to be creative in your description of your features, but do not go so far as to tell them the color and dimensions of each room because that leaves little to the imagination. You want the potential buyer to come and view the home.

Next, list features of your neighborhood or community, including phrases like:

- Top school system in the state

- Neighborhood swimming pool
- Minutes from interstate, shopping, and dining

After this information, list the price of the home. The only other thing you might consider including on the flier is the address of the website or blog site you have set up for your home. You do not need much more information than this on a flier because this is enough to encourage buyers to visit and take a look. You have given enough information to eliminate unnecessary calls from buyers who either need more or less than what your home has to offer. You will also attract buyers looking for a home in your price range by including the listing price on the flier.

The Internet

The internet is your most important tool when it comes to marketing your home. In addition to your MLS listing, it is very beneficial to set up a blog or website for your home. Doing this is much easier and cheaper than you may think. By creating a presence on the Web, you are reaching significantly more people and more potential buyers than with advertising in your community and local paper.

A blog is the easiest and most affordable way to create Web presence for your home. A blog is a type of website, usually maintained by an individual with regular entries of commentary, descriptions of events, or other material such as graphics or video.

The easiest blog platforms to use are *Blogger* (**www.blogger.com**) and *WordPress* (**http://wordpress.org**). To use Blogger, you will have to set up a Gmail email address. You can simply use this email address as your official house marketing address. You do not have to create a Gmail account before creating a blog; when you create the blog it will automatically create an account for you.

To create the blog, visit **www.blogger.com** and click on "create a blog" from the home page. From there, you will be prompted to enter basic information, and it will then create a blog for you with this information. Once you have set up the blog, you will begin to create the design of the site and add content in the layout section. Click on the layout tab and it will bring you to where you can create a header add pictures of your house by clicking on "add gadget." You can also add a map to your house.

Setting up a Gmail email account: When you visit **www.gmail. com**, there is a link at the bottom right side of the page that enables you to create a Gmail account. Once you click "create an account," you will be prompted to enter basic information and create a username and password to access your account. Consider creating a name that relates specifically to your house as your user name. For instance, use "houseforsale" or "orchard-streethouse" as your user name, and Gmail will automatically attach "@gmail.com."

Additionally, you can use the add-gadget option to add links to the local school system, community center, restaurants, and entertainment. You can post the specifics of the house by clicking on the "post" tab and that will bring you to a title and text box where you can put your catchy headline phrase and then in the text box you can type all the information about the house that you included on the flier.

Once you have your blog up and running, e-mail the link to the site to all your friends, family, and coworkers, asking them to forward it to everyone they know. Using people you already know to market your home is an easy way to create a viral marketing campaign for almost no cost.

Photographing Your Home

The importance of photographs of your home cannot be underestimated. Buyers searching on the internet will often choose which homes to inquire about further and look at in person based on pictures alone. If your pictures are not reflective of your home, and do not accurately depict your home, you are at a big disadvantage.

The biggest problem with pictures is often that sellers take them themselves, and they do not invest the time or money to either hire a professional photographer or research how to take better photos. Usually, photos that are not taken in the right lighting from the right angle either make the house look too dark or too narrow.

The other mistake sellers often make with pictures is putting a picture of every room in the house on the internet. Avoid this, since it is rare that every room in your home will have every single feature a buyer is looking for, but usually even the rooms that do not can be modified slightly with paint or minor improvements to meet a buyer's needs. If a potential buyer is clicking through the pictures, many of them could be great. If the buyer comes across the one room in your home that is not updated — for instance, it still has wood paneling on the walls — he or she may dismiss your home and click on the next option because one picture was not what he or she was looking for. Your goal is to entice buyers to come and look at the house in person to decide if it is for them because most houses look much better than the amateur pictures on the internet.

If you are concerned about how the rooms you have selected will come across on camera, or if there is an area of the room you do not want to highlight, take an up-close shot of an excellent feature of the room, such as the amazing fireplace or the beautifully stained cabinets.

Because you want to encourage buyers to come to your open house or call you for a private viewing, you want to entice them with a limited amount of high quality photographs of the best rooms in your home. Four should suffice in addition to a front view picture and perhaps one of the backyard. Ideally, these four would include the kitchen, living room, master bedroom, and master bathroom. You do not need to include pictures of every closet and the laundry room. They can see those when they get there to view the home.

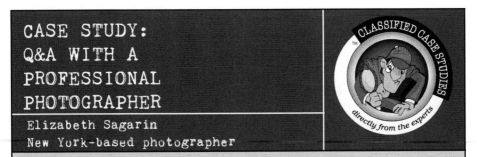

CASE STUDY: Q&A WITH A PROFESSIONAL PHOTOGRAPHER

Elizabeth Sagarin
New York-based photographer

Elizabeth Sagarin is a New York-based photographer with more than 15 years of experience. Her work has appeared in a number of arts, lifestyle, and fashion publications as well as *Newsday*, a regional New York newspaper. She is also a successful wedding and event photographer. The following is her advice on taking the best photos of your home that will present it in the best possible light and help you successfully attract a buyer.

What is your general take on photographing a home?

Over the past ten years, my photographic experiences have run the gamut. Homes, like people, have certain character and charm. However, homes are not able to smile or do an animated gesture, which usually makes a photo stand out. So, it may take a bit to figure out a way to elicit character from a home. That treasure hunt is part of the challenge, but also part of the fun. Make it a goal of yours to a have selective vision that seeks out the positive aspects in a home.

What is the best light to photograph in?

Daylight is the easiest and most reliable source of light for any subject. Fussing with flash or ambient light can put a real damper on things. And most people are not equipped with the necessary equipment to artificially light an interior properly. You can do this easily by opening the shades.

What is the best time of day to photograph outside?

Take pictures when there are no harsh shadows. The best time is usually during the morning when the sun is low in the sky, or during the late afternoon. The light is more evenly distributed across the face or surface of a subject, which makes for a uniform exposure across the entire picture.

When the sun is high in the sky with no cloud coverage, it has a tendency to beam down on only parts of the house and be completely absent from others. So get up early or get outside before the sun goes down and take advantage of the day's best lighting. You will experience something photographers like to call the "magic hour," when everything has a magical glow about it.

During an overcast day, you might be able to take a proper picture in the middle of the day because the clouds will diffuse the light of the sun.

What is the best way to use natural light indoors?

Again, your main objective here is to have light evenly distributed throughout the space. When using natural light indoors, you want to do so in a way that does not make one part of the room very bright and the other much darker, otherwise you will have to use some sort of artificial lighting source to balance out.

A severe lighting contrast from one side of a room to another can occur if the light source is coming from only one side of the space. On the other hand, having windows on all sides of a room helps to balance out a room, but this is not typical. However, if there are windows evenly distributed around a room, then adjust them accordingly whether through blinds or shades, so they cast a balanced amount of light from one side of the room to the other. Sometimes windows on a single side of a room are enough to light an entire room, especially if they are high and low on the wall. In that case, use this to your advantage and set up your camera in a spot that highlights such a room's assets.

Certain times of the day as well as certain conditions can yield better results for indoor photography as well. Overcast skies are good for producing even lighting throughout the course of a day, which can be useful when trying to light an entire room evenly. Simply open the shades and let the light pour in. The diffused light will subtly bath the room in an all-over glow.

The same advice goes for morning and late afternoon light; it is not as harsh and therefore can more uniformly light a room. Play up the fact there are windows in a room — that is a selling feature. Use them as a tool in lighting the room itself as well as feature them integral part of the room that complements the overall space.

What is the best way to use artificial light while photographing indoors?

Artificial lighting should be distributed evenly throughout a room. Those features you want to have more prominence in the picture should be accented with a slightly brighter appearance than other parts. For instance, lights above a fireplace should be a little brighter to attract the eye to what is most import. Overall, the lighting should not vary much. Lighting that is high, low, and mid-level is ideal. It should not come from just one direction. No matter the room, every nook and cranny should be visible to the viewer.

What are the best ways to feature positive aspects of a subject while minimizing negative ones?

If you do not want certain aspects of your home seen, do not show them. Do not take pictures of the bad, only the good. Do your best to crop out those aspects that you do not want seen in a logical manner. If the crop makes the overall picture awkward or clearly manipulated in a way to exclude something, the viewer will know something is amiss and discredit your picture and ultimately what you're selling. Focus on the positive if need be. Every picture does not have to show the totality of a room. Little scenarios can be just as effective, if not more effective when trying to give people an idea of what they are in for.

What are the best angles to take a photo from to make a room look larger?

Pick a vantage point from which you can capture most of the room with your camera to accentuate the size of the room. Usually the view from the doorway is a good place to start. Position yourself in the doorway and zoom out the lens of the camera to get as much of the room in view as possible. Sometimes positioning the camera from a slightly higher angle can help get a room in view. Always shoot from a position that goes from the side of the entryway. Shooting toward the doorway can compress a room and make people want to leave.

What are some ways to make a photo unique, or stand out?

Good photos with interesting subject matter stand out. Well-lit and nicely composed shots are a sure-fire way to get people's attention. Including colorful elements such as flowers or artwork in a room is a solid strategy when trying to get people to look.

What kind of camera would you recommend for a novice user that is easy to use, fairly inexpensive, and decent quality?

Nowadays there are so many digital point-and-shoot cameras on the market capable of producing quality photos at a reasonable price that you practically cannot go wrong with any of the name brand offerings out today. The camera should have quality optics, a variable zoom capable of shooting at wide angles, and have at least 8mbs of capture quality. Budget around $300 to $4000 to get such a camera. Whether to go digital or not should not even be a question at this point — digital is the format you want. You will be able to keep shooting until you get it right without wasting film or money or really that much time.

What size should a picture be for a clear download to the Internet? (What size is a high-resolution photo?)

Photos on the Web should not be more than 1 megabyte to ensure fast downloading and easy viewing from any browser. Most cameras shoot at 300 dpi (dots per inch) and produce a file that is too large for Web use. However, you should shoot your picture at the highest setting then reduce later in an imaging software program. Most, if not all, consumer cameras on the market today come with additional imaging software so do not worry about purchasing additions. Most are very user-friendly. Some even offer presets that reduce pictures specifically for use on the Web. So when considering a camera, take into account the supplemental software and do not get caught up in too many features — optics, file size, and focal length are the most important.

What other general photography tips do you have?

Bend your knees, go high, and then go low. Repeatedly try to get a good shot. Use a tripod if necessary. Take your time and a deep breath. Move around. Experiment and have fun. It is only a matter of time before you get the shot you want.

Word-of-Mouth Marketing

According to the website The Truth About FSBO: Complete Selling System, at **www.truthaboutfsbo.com**, more than one-third of FSBO sellers sell to someone they already know. This statistic emphasizes the importance of word-of-mouth marketing in addition to traditional marketing. Word-of-mouth marketing is particularly important for FSBO sellers because sellers must do the marketing work a Realtor would and the easiest way to do this is to use the networks you already have in place.

Creating Your Network:

You probably know more people than you think you do, and therefore you have potential for being one of those one-third of FSBO sellers who sell to someone they know. Think about all the different groups within your network by writing down as many people's names as you can in 30 seconds. From there, take another two minutes to write down five more people under each of those 10 people that those 10 people know. Be sure to include people like your pharmacist, doctor, grocery store cashier, dry cleaner, and favorite restaurant's waitress.

Your network includes more than just your friends. It includes co-workers, acquaintances, friends of friends, fellow parishioners, neighbors, family members, your children's teachers, and parents of their friends. Think of your network as anyone you know or *may* know through someone else. It is not about who *you* know sometimes, it may be about whom your network knows. A teacher at your daughter's school may know a friend whose mother is looking for a condominium in your neighborhood. Getting the word to everyone in your network is very important, and all this involves is telling everyone you can that your house is on the market. Invite them to come to you next open house.

Handling Phone Calls

Handling the phone calls inquiring about your house may be challenging if you do not take the time to set up a system to manage this. Dedicate a separate phone line for taking calls about the house, which will allow you to set up a professional voicemail message for the phone line asking callers to leave a message. Be sure to include a realistic time frame in which you will return the caller's call.

Your goal should be to take as many calls as possible, but you should only take a call when you are able to talk. If you are in a loud place, on the other line, or in between meetings with only a minute to talk, let the call go to voicemail. Just be sure to return the call as soon as possible. Each missed call is a potential missed opportunity to sell, and you want to catch callers when they are most interested in your house, which is when they make that first phone call to you. When you do answer your phone about inquiries, you want to be professional and polite. Prepare a short description of your house that you can memorize to repeat to each caller.

Do not automatically jump into a long speech about the house. It may deter buyers, and you may waste your time giving information the potential buyer does not need. It is quite common that what a buyer really wants to know is whether your house has one particular feature they are looking for; so letting her initiate the conversation is a good idea. If she does not have any particular questions, ask her where she learned about the listing if she has not already mentioned this.

The goal is to play up the features of your house without overwhelming the caller. For instance, if she asks you about the size of the backyard and you have a huge backyard with a built-in barbecue, fire pit, and large patio area, then tell her how much you and your family enjoy cookouts in the backyard.

If you have an open house scheduled in the next week of the call, invite the caller to come to the open house. Better yet, invite the caller for a private showing at a time that is convenient for her. Offer directions to your house. You want to make the experience as convenient and easy for her as possible, which is why it is important to accommodate all potential buyers as much as possible.

Chapter 9

Running an Open House

O pen houses will be a critical part of your marketing process. They enable a large volume of people to come in and out of your home at their own pace and convenience, and they expose your home to potential buyers, in addition to your neighbors and Realtors who may bring you buyers as well.

Typically, open houses are held on Sunday afternoons between 2 and 5 p.m. Although you can technically hold an open house any day of the week, Sunday is the day when most buyers are out visiting open houses and searching for homes on the market. People tend to plan an afternoon of looking at open houses in advance, and they are commonly held on Sundays, when a buyer can usually visit several in one afternoon.

It is important that you keep hosting open houses, even if you only get a few people each time, and that you stay open for the entire time your sign says you will be open.

To market your open house, there are a few things you can do:

- Post the date and time on your blog
- Email the information to all of your friends and ask them to forward to theirs
- Place fliers on bulletin boards all over town
- Notify Realtors if you are willing to work with one
- Run a line ad in the real estate section of your local newspaper
- Put your sign up the Thursday before the open house with balloons
- Place directional open house signs

Take your open house signs down on Sunday after the open house is over, even if you plan to do it again the following Sunday. Leaving them up will only cause passersby to think the sign is for the open house you already had and you forgot to take the sign down.

Remember to capitalize on another open house's marketing if you plan to hold yours on the same day.

Your house should be ready for the open house for the most part if you have already done all of the de-cluttering, repairs, cleaning, and staging. Beyond marketing and fixing the house, it is always a good idea to bake cookies just before the open house and offer them to buyers.

Finally, have extra fliers ready and sitting out by your cookies for buyers to take and then have your open house logbook sitting out as well, with a pen, so you can keep buyers updated on price changes. If they do not want to give the information, then do not press them for it. If visitors leave contact information, add them to your e-mail database and forward them a reminder email in the weeks following their visit that the house is still available. Ask them to tell their friends and co-workers about the next open house. Be sure to keep this email standard and professional, and do not send more than one or two emails. If you do not hear back from someone, do not continue to email.

Marketing Your Open House and Creating Traffic

There are little things you can do to take advantage of events going on around you, in your neighborhood and community, to help you maximize your marketing.

For example, in garage sale season, almost every neighborhood holds neighborhood garage sales, and when yours does, this is the perfect time do some extra marketing. You can put out extra fliers or even hold your house open during this time. You may get a number of people who are looking just for the fun of it and you will be busy trying to keep up with the traffic keep everything clean but it is a wonderful chance to get extra exposure.

If you are willing to pay a Realtor a commission for bringing you a buyer, contact all your local real estate firms and invite agents from these firms to come to your open house. Your goal is to create as much traffic as possible to gain the most exposure.

Be sure and ask everyone who comes through to remember your house if they happen to come across anyone who is interested in buying a home. Other opportunities to take advantage of would be anything going on in your community, such as a local fair, parade, or festival of any kind.

You can use this opportunity to pass out fliers to everyone at the event, place extra fliers around town, and even set up a small booth. Having refreshments, cookies, and snacks will always help your cause and create a welcoming, inviting feeling for everyone who walks into your house.

Handling Individual Showings

It can be nerve-racking to have strangers in your home, whether this is for an open house or a private showing. Although you should not worry excessively about safety, you should be aware of the potential for theft during an open house, and be cautious about personal safety during a private showing.

The best way to avoid theft is to store all your personal belongings and valuables in a safe area that is not accessible during an open house. Since you will not be able to monitor everyone that comes through your house during an open house, it is important you feel comfortable with strangers in rooms of your house when you are not present.

When you are showing your home, always carry your cell phone with you so you can access it immediately if necessary.

Besides storing valuables, the best way to ensure safety and comfort is to have multiple people at your open house that can help you monitor guests. Ask a friend, family member, or neighbor you trust to help take visitors through the house. This will make visitors feel as though they are getting a personal tour while providing you with the comfort of having other people in the house you trust.

Effectively Showing Your Home

When you are about to show a house, first clear out the family and put away all the pets. Pick one of the adults to stay behind and show the house. If the whole family is there, the potential buyers will likely not feel completely comfortable to look as they wish and ask questions. They may feel as if they are imposing or they may be very private and simply are not the type to be themselves in front of strangers. All of this could cause the showing to not go as well as it might if the buyers had the peace and the space to look through the house.

A tour of your house should begin with a warm greeting. As soon as buyers come to the door and you open it, greet them with your name and a handshake. Invite them in and initiate a conversation with them. Be very positive and upbeat; professional but personable. Sample questions to initiate a conversation include:

- Did you find the house all right?
- Do you live in the area?
- Thank you for coming, are you ready to tour the house?

The tour should follow the natural flow of your house that should be pre-determined for each guest. Begin with the closest room to the front door, most likely the living room. Be specific about each room, describing the room's special features. You can include anecdotal information like what you like best about your home, or how great the living room is for entertaining. The stories will inject a personal aspect to each room, tapping into a buyer's emotions.

Take guests through each room in your house and wait for them to be ready to see the next room and move on. Give them time to visit each room and get a feel for it, and to ask any questions they may have. Instead of walking out of a room first, let them walk out first or you can ask them if they are ready to see the next room.

Show the entire inside of the house first, the first floor and then the second floor if you have one, and then ask if guests want to see the garage, the yard, or the basement. Continue to highlight the features of each room, which could include:

- Large bedroom closets
- Big bay windows in the living room
- Room for a large dining room table in the dining room
- New appliances in the kitchen

Following Up

After the showing, follow up at least once. Call the potential buyer and ask him what he thought of the house. He may say he liked it and is still deciding — or, he loved it but he is not quite ready to make an offer. On the other hand, the buyer may insinuate he did not like your house and in this case, get some feedback; it could help you make an improvement that you otherwise missed, better preparing you for the next potential buyer.

When you call to follow up, thank him for visiting your house and ask what he thought of it. If you sense the buyer is not interested, be polite and do not be pushy. Simply thank him for visiting and hang up. Invite him to spread the word about the listing.

If Your Home Is Not Selling

If your home is not selling, it is most likely for one of three reasons: it is overpriced, there is a feature of your home that is not attractive, or your house is absent of an important feature such as a second bathroom.

The most common problem with FSBOs that do not sell is overpricing. If your house is overpriced, you will usually not get much traffic at an open house or requests for private showings. On the other hand, if you are getting a lot of traffic at open houses and requests for private showings but no callbacks or requests for second viewings, chances are either there is something turning off the buyers about your house, or your house is missing something buyers want and need.

A dirty, cluttered home turns off most buyers, so consider this may be the problem if you are not getting a good response from your open houses. If your house is outdated, perhaps with dirty carpets or an older kitchen, consider making minimal upgrades. Often, the lack of a second bathroom or a bathroom on the first floor will turn off buyers. This highlights the importance of knowing your market and what is for sale in your neighborhood before you put your own house on the market.

Chapter 10

Handling Offers and Working with Buyers

I deally, you want as many offers as possible to drive up the sales price of your house. The more offers, the more demand and competition and competition drives up the price of an item.

Handling offers can be confusing, especially if you are eager to sell and do not want to negotiate. A buyer will most likely make an offer that is below asking price. Some will offer a few thousand below, and some may offer a significantly lower number than your asking price. You should determine a number you are comfortable selling for before you list your house, and this will give you some room to negotiate quickly and effectively without causing you to scramble to figure out if you can afford to take a lower offer.

Getting an offer is only the beginning of the process and you should not consider an offer a guarantee that the buyer will purchase your house. There are several factors that come into play after you receive an offer on a house, including a buyer's qualifications, the amount of the offer, and how many offers you receive.

In order to be official, an offer should be in writing in the form of an Offer to Purchase contract that the buyer or buyer's real estate agent should present you with. Once you sign the offer, you are accepting it and creating a legal contract, binding you to the sale.

Determining if a Buyer Is Qualified

As soon as you receive an offer from a buyer, it is imperative to determine whether that buyer is qualified to purchase your home before you go any further. You do not want to discover this three weeks into the process. You can avoid this by having a mortgage broker or lender present at your open house to qualify buyers on the spot, or by immediately referring buyers to a specific mortgage lender you have already identified for the purpose.

If a buyer is aggressive about purchasing, he will likely bring with him a pre-qualification or pre-approval letter to an open house or showing. A pre-approval letter is ideal because it means the buyer has already met with a lender and the lender has reviewed the buyer's finances and determined what the buyer can afford. Pre-qualification simply means the lender has stated a buyer is qualified for a loan, but the lender has not reviewed the buyer's financials to determine an amount the buyer can afford.

Having a mortgage lender on site can be extremely beneficial, not only to qualify people on the spot — which can speed up the process — but also to answer any questions a potential buyer may have and give you tips on the general process.

Managing Multiple Offers

According to the National Association of Realtors, real estate agents must adhere to a code of ethics when it comes to managing multiple offers. The association stipulates that agents should:

- Submit offers as quickly as possible and not withhold any offer from a potential buyer from the seller
- Submit offers and counter-offers until the sale has been closed
- Respond honestly to inquiries from anyone about an offer
- Refrain from intentionally creating a bidding war or falsifying bids to drive up the selling price

As a FSBO seller, you should adhere to these guidelines as well. You want to be honest and open with all potential buyers without revealing too much. While multiple offers is good and can drive up the sales price of your house, most buyers do not want to get involved in a bidding war and you may lose potential buyers if you allow the bidding process to get out of hand. The best strategy in handling multiple offers is to reveal to all bidders that there are other offers on the table without revealing the amount of the bid. Accept the bid that is closest to your asking price. Getting greedy and hoping for a price higher than your asking price can back fire and turn off buyers.

Working With Buyers and Their Realtors

If you have made it known that you will pay a commission to a buyer's agent for bringing you a buyer who purchases your home, be open to Realtors calling you to bring potential buyers to see your house.

You can be present when the Realtor comes to view the house with their buyer, but many times a Realtor will request that you leave. This is common — you can stay until the buyer arrives, then let them in and visit a neighbor until you see they are gone. Or, you can leave a key in a previously discussed location to allow the Realtor and buyer to enter the house while you are not there.

Allow them a minimum of 45 minutes to show the house before returning. You can also ask the Realtor to call you when they are done so you when to return home.

Do not discuss specific information regarding the house or your financial matters with a Realtor you do not want to partner with. If a Realtor or buyer asks questions, then tell him you have a set of disclosures that you will be glad to provide. You are not required to disclose personal information, nor should you. This is usually an attempt to find out how low you will go on the price or how desperate you are to sell. Answering these questions will compromise your selling position.

Buyers, naturally, will look for the best deal. Any information, like what you paid for the house or your incentive for selling the house, will likely alert them to possible desperation to sell on your part. They may take advantage of it and may offer you a low amount. If you are trying to short sell your house, you should alert the buyer since he will need to do extra steps to buy the house. Use your discretion.

If you are trying to avoid losing your house to foreclosure and you are up against a timeline, consider informing any serious buyers of this so they know there is a deadline. The goal is to make the transaction as smooth and convenient as possible for all parties involved, which may involve compromise on your part as well as theirs. Being too demanding may turn off a buyer, while being a pushover and allowing them to dictate the process may be detrimental to you. The key is finding a middle ground with compromising.

After you receive the offer in writing and sign it, you have obligated yourself to selling your house to that buyer. Accepting the Offer to Purchase initiates the process, which involves a series of additional steps and paperwork. Once you accept a buyer's offer, it is time for the buyer to get a mortgage, get an inspection, and make an earnest money deposit.

Earnest Money Deposits and Escrow Companies

An earnest money deposit is a deposit a buyer will give to you to demonstrate he is serious about purchasing your house, also known as a "good faith" deposit. There is no set amount required for an earnest money deposit and the amount will depend on the market. In a seller's market, buyers will likely put down less than they would in a competitive buyer's market. In a seller's market, a buyer would want to give more of an incentive to the seller to accept his offer if there are multiple offers. In a buyer's market, there will be less competition among buyers and therefore the buyer has less of an incentive to provide a large earnest money deposit.

An earnest money deposit gives you assurance you have a serious buyer and gives you an incentive to take the house off the market, cease showings and marketing, and proceed with the contract to closing. If for some reason the buyer backs out, you could potentially lose precious selling time and other possible buyers during the time your house is off the market. Buyers put up earnest money to show they are willing to risk something as well in order to complete the transaction. If they have nothing to lose should they change their minds, it would be much easier for them to walk away from the contract had they not put up earnest money.

A typical earnest money deposit is between one and three percent, but it varies by state and market. In some states like California, an earnest money deposit is required to make the contract valid and to initiate the selling process.

Although it may seem logical, you should never offer to hold an earnest money deposit for a buyer; this is the role of an escrow company. An escrow company specializes in being a third and independent party to hold funds involved in a real estate transaction. When a buyer deposits money to an escrow company, the company deposits the funds into an escrow bank account where the funds stay until the company releases them at the request of the mortgage lender when the sale closes.

After you have received an earnest money deposit, it is time to begin the process of drafting your sales contract, creating seller's disclosures, and gathering other necessary tax documents.

Your Closing Timeline and Costs

The amount of time it will take to close on your property will depend on how smoothly each part of the process goes. The ideal time frame in which to accept an offer and close on the property is 45 to 60 days, but it can take longer depending on possible hold ups. Hold ups can result from problems with the title discovered during the title search, back taxes, or liens due on the property you were not aware of, or problems with the buyer getting qualified for a loan.

If you are on a tight schedule and need to move in a specific period of time, be sure to allow extra time, at least two weeks, for hold ups in the closing process.

Closing costs are costs that are associated with closing a real estate deal. They typically range from two to five percent of the sale price of the house. As the seller, you will not have to pay for things like the inspection fee and the mortgage fees, but you will be responsible for a few costs like any property taxes or homeowner's association fees you owe. The following closing costs vary depending on the specifics of your transaction — such as if you are offering to pay for a portion of closing costs. You may also, for instance, decide to offer your buyer a home warranty as part of your negotiations, which you would then be responsible for paying.

Costs typically paid by the buyer:

- Lender fees, including a mortgage initiation fee
- Appraisal fee as required by the lender
- Property insurance
- Inspection fees
- Home warranty fees

Costs typically paid by the seller:

- Any Realtor fees
- Escrow fees
- Property taxes, usually pro-rated
- Any homeowner's association dues, pro-rated
- Legal and attorney fees

Negotiable fees that can be paid by either party:

- Title fees
- Fees for recording the deed to the house
- Property transfer taxes
- Survey of the land fees

Offering a Seller's Concession

Many sellers, particularly when buyers are scarce, will offer seller concessions — something a seller gives up as an incentive to the buyer. Concessions are usually financial, in the form of a percentage of the closing costs.

For example, say your home is listed for $300,000 and you receive an offer for $280,000. You will most likely want to counter-offer to get a higher price, unless you are satisfied with the offer and willing to accept it. Instead of counter offering just a number, like $290,000, you can counter offer $295,000 with an offer to pay all or a portion of closing costs. This means the buyer would pay $295,000 and you would pay a percentage of the closing costs at closing. This percentage is up to you; typically seller's concessions are no more than three percent of the sale price, but can be higher or lower depending on the market. In a buyer's market, you may have to work harder and offer a higher concession to attract a buyer.

Using these numbers as an example, you would not want to offer more than $8,850 worth of concessions (three percent of the sale price). You should always include a clause in your contract regarding the specific concessions you have agreed on.

Concessions can also be helpful for repairs and problems with the house. If you know your house needs a new roof, for example, or if your entire house is outdated and you know you will have a problem selling it, you can offer to pay a percentage of the closing costs to compensate for this, or you can offer a lower sales price. This gives the buyer an incentive to purchase the house despite its downfalls.

Chapter **11**

Handling Contracts and Other Documents

The legal and contractual aspects of your FSBO transactions are obviously of great importance. As with any real estate deal, you do not want any loose ends to come back to haunt you in the future. However, there is no reason to think that sound legal practices will run up your costs significantly. In fact, this book includes a CD with examples of contracts that are relevant in your FSBO transaction. This chapter discusses the essentials.

The Contract

The sales contract, also known as the sales and purchase agreement, is the most important document in your transaction. It will stipulate all the details of the sale and outline a timeline as well as specific requirements to complete the sale.

A sales contract usually includes the following:

- The names of the buyers and seller
- Contact information for both parties
- The address of the property
- The property's description, including details such as square footage and lot size
- Any items included in the sale: such as furniture, fixtures like door knobs and chandeliers, and any blinds or drapery on the windows
- The closing date for the sale
- The amount of the earnest money deposit
- Any required disclosures, which include seller's disclosure and lead paint and radon disclosures
- A timeline for a buyer to get a home inspection
- A timeline for a buyer to be approved for a mortgage
- A date the offer expires should either party fault on any requirements or deadlines
- Any stipulations provided by the buyer's lender, such as appraisal requirements
- A timeline for the buyer to do a final walk though of the property

Anything you put in the contract and sometimes what you leave out of the contract is enforceable by law. You want to create a contract that is solid and requires both you and the buyer to uphold individual obligations.

The CD-ROM accompanying this book includes an easy-to-use boilerplate contract. Be sure to review the contract thoroughly and add in clauses that are specific to your sale.

A mistake many FSBO sellers make is using a boilerplate contract without adding any clauses, such as a timeline for a buyer to get an inspection for instance, that speak to the specifics of your transaction. The contract should protect your interests as the seller while outlining your obligations and holding both parties accountable for their respective obligations.

The contract should cover not only the legal and common address of the property but of course specific dates things should happen, as well as the printed names and signatures of each person involved in the transaction. If a married couple decides to sell, then both the husband and wife should sign the contract. This applies to the buyers as well. The contract should include a specific closing date and timeline for inspections, repairs, and anything else that is to be done.

A "mortgage commitment" is the loan approval from the mortgage company, and it will stipulate any conditions that still need to be cleared in order for borrower to obtain the loan. The contract should stipulate that these conditions be met within seven days of contract acceptance.

You should also have an agreed-upon repair cap in case something unexpected arises during an inspection. The clause would read something like this: "Seller agrees to make repairs called for by home inspector or appraiser, up to $1,000. If repairs required by an inspector or appraiser exceed $1,000 both buyer and seller have the option to renegotiate the contract."

You should include a clause that specifically addressed what will come with the sale and what will not be included. This is important for anything you want to reserve besides your furniture and belongings that are not considered attached to the property. It is generally assumed that appliances such as a stove will stay with the property when it is sold, so include similar items. The clause would read something like this: "Seller reserves all window treatments including blinds, swing set in backyard, hot tub, and stove."

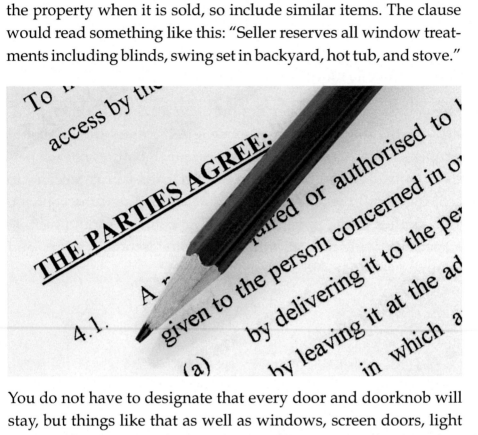

You do not have to designate that every door and doorknob will stay, but things like that as well as windows, screen doors, light fixtures, built-in microwaves, and cabinet doors will stay unless you reserve them. Blinds generally stay as well, so if you wish to take them, include it in the reservation clause.

You will also include a clause about the earnest money deposit and where you want to close the property. Earnest money, by law, must be held in an escrow account. Ask the title company to hold it in their escrow account so you do not have to open a separate account just for the transaction. If you want to require the earnest money be nonrefundable, stipulate that in the contract. You should also stipulate where the buyer should make the deposit, which is usually to a title or escrow company.

Contingencies

Either party involved in the sale of your house may request various contingencies be included in the contract. A contingency is a type of clause that releases either a buyer or a seller from the obligations of the contract should certain requirements not be met. Contingencies are beneficial for both you and the buyer because they provide a safe and legal exit for either in case certain conditions are not met.

For example, your buyer may have to sell his house before buying yours, but he wants to go ahead and write a contract. In the contract, you may want to include a contingency that states something similar to this: "The sale of property located at 500 West Jane Street, Funville, Utah, is contingent upon the sale of buyer's property located at 200 West John Street, Happyville, Utah."

Other contingencies speak to specific issues like:

- The appraisal
- The home inspection
- A radon, mold, and asbestos inspection
- A lead paint inspection
- The results of the title report

These contingencies would stipulate that the sale is contingent on, or will be made "as long as" these issues are met. A buyer will likely want to include a contingency for the above inspections and the appraisal, which would allow them to terminate the contract should a significant problem arise during inspections or should the appraiser find the house is worth $20,000 less than its listing price.

As the seller, you are also able to include contingencies. For instance, if you must secure a new job before you can move and sell your house, you would want to include a contingency that states the sale is contingent upon you getting a new job. If you include a contingency, be sure to include in the contract that the house will remain on the market until the condition is met. Include that you will continue to accept back up offers during the time the contingency is in place, and should you get an offer, the buyers have a set amount of time to remove the contingency. The time frame in which the buyer can remove the contingency is negotiable and should be decided upon before the contract is signed. Include a clause in your contract that stipulates the time frame for a removal of contingencies. When the buyer signs a form that states he or she hereby agrees to remove said contingency, effective immediately, the contingency can be removed.

The biggest risk for you as the seller occurs when your buyer must sell his house before purchasing yours. In this case, it is essential to include a contingency, with a time frame, that outlines that the sale is contingent on the closing of the buyer's current home. Keep in mind, however, that if the buyer's sale does not close for some reason, your deal may fall through. You can request information on their contract, such as a qualification letter from both their lender and their buyer's lender.

All of these statements, agreements, and "exits" that are defined within the contract are called contract clauses. If you are using a boilerplate contract, such as the one included with this book, be sure to add what clauses you need to the contract before signing anything. Handling the paperwork and drawing up the contract are often the most challenging parts of the process for a FSBO seller. Many do not feel comfortable drafting and reviewing a contract. If you are not 100 percent comfortable with handling the contract and other paperwork yourself, consider hiring a real estate attorney or a service to handle this for you.

A real estate attorney will charge you a fee to review and edit your contract and other legal documents. The best way to find a reputable attorney is to ask for a recommendation from someone you know. You can also check with your state's bar association or visit Real Estate Lawyers.com at **www.realestatelawyers.com** to search for a real estate attorney in your specific area.

The other option is to enlist a company such as Assist-2-Sell (**www.assist2sell.com**) or HouseSavvy (**www.housesavvy.com**) to handle the paperwork for you. Both companies, along with many other discount brokerages, offer a "paperwork only" service that is either billed as a flat fee or a percentage of your sale price. For this fee, the company will handle everything to do with the legal paperwork. HouseSavvy charges a fee of one percent of the sale price, which includes negotiations with the buyer, preparation and review of the Offer to Purchase and the Purchase and Sale Agreement, coordination of escrow, and the closing. In essence, the company serves as not only your real estate attorney but also your closing agent and escrow company.

The Importance of a Home Warranty

A home warranty is similar to an insurance policy on your home. It covers the repair and replacement costs of a variety of issues with systems like the central air conditioning, heating, plumbing, electrical, and sewage system; and issues with standard appliances and equipment. Coverage varies significantly across warranty companies. A home warranty contract does not cover all home repairs, or anything related to the structure of the house. Roof damage, for instance, is not covered by a home warranty.

You are not obligated to provide a home warranty for a buyer, but it will provide a layer of protection for you should something go wrong with an appliance or system within the first year of the buyer's homeownership. For example, if you close on the house and within three weeks the stove breaks, the home warranty would cover this. If you did not have a warranty, the buyer may call you and demand a replacement. With a home warranty and an agreement that the buyer will pay the deductible, the problem is fixed with a phone call to the insuring company.

The cost for a home warranty is usually around $350 to $500 for one year of coverage, and $100 to $300 more for additional warranty protection. The deductible is often about $100. Most home warranty companies have extra coverage for items such as hot tubs and swimming pools for an additional cost. Some home warranties are better than others, but research the different providers, call them, and ask for references so you can measure customer satisfaction. Better yet, let the buyer pick his own provider. Be sure to include the existence of a home warranty in the contract with a clause stating something like this: "seller to provide a home warranty service of the buyer's choosing at a cost not to exceed $450, buyer to pay deductible."

Understanding the Legalities

Seller's disclosures

Seller disclosures are forms that a seller fills out to disclose certain facts about property. A Property Condition Disclosure, which is included in the accompanying CD-ROM, is the general disclosure form required in most states. It includes questions about the property relating to its condition, problems, and issues of hazardous materials.

Not every state requires seller's disclosures, but more than 32 do and federal law states that a lead paint disclosure must be included if your house was built prior to 1978. Other commonly required disclosures include a radon disclosure and an asbestos disclosure. Radon is a hazardous gas that is known to cause lung cancer, and asbestos is a mineral that was used in construction materials when it was not known to be hazardous.

To research the requirements of your state and to download disclosure forms specific to your state, visit U.S. Legal Forms, Inc., at **www.uslegalforms.com**. The website charges a fee for the disclosures, which you have the option of being delivered via e-mail or standard mail. If you are unsure of what is required or want to confirm with a professional, contact a title company or real estate attorney in your state and confirm you are complying with state law. If you work with an attorney or a company to handle your paperwork, they will tell you what forms you need.

In most states, sellers are required to disclose every known defect about the property. It is important to be honest on these forms. If you have concerns over an issue that you cannot do anything about, just disclose the issue. There is always the option of making a concession in the price to help compensate for the defect.

Seller disclosures can include any the following and the requirements vary by state:

- Property condition disclosure (the basic form required that includes detailed information about each room, system, and aspect of your house)
- Lead-based paint disclosure
- Asbestos disclosure
- Radon disclosure
- Hazardous material disclosure

- Nuisance or noise disclosure
- Use of synthetic building materials disclosure
- Mudslide, avalanche, earthquake, or natural disaster disclosure
- Presence of ghosts disclosure
- Wildlife hazard disclosure

If you have a concern over the condition of your house and possible defects that you may not be aware of, it is in your best interest to hire a good, credible, and reputable home inspector to perform an inspection and give you accurate information as to the condition of the house. This way you are covered and can disclose more accurately. A good home inspection will run between $270 and $300, if your house is average in size and condition. This price can vary based on size or additional amenities like a sprinkler system or pool. The investment is worth it particularly if your home is older and you think you may come across issues that the buyer's inspector may find.

Fair housing laws

According to the U.S. Department of Housing and Urban Development (HUD), The Fair Housing Act of 1968 "prohibits discrimination in the sale, rental, and financing of dwellings, and in other housing-related transactions, based on race, color, national origin, religion, sex, familial status (including children under the age of 18 living with parents or legal custodians, pregnant women, people securing custody of children under the age of 18), and handicap (disability)."

According to HUD.com (**www.hud.com**), which is not affiliated with the U.S. Department of Housing and Urban Development, "In the Sale and Rental of Housing: No one may take any of the following actions based on race, color, national origin, religion, sex, familial status, or handicap:

- Refuse to rent or sell housing
- Refuse to negotiate for housing
- Make housing unavailable
- Deny a dwelling
- Set different terms, conditions, or privileges for sale or rental of a dwelling
- Falsely deny that housing is available for inspection, sale, or rental
- For profit, persuade owners to sell or rent (blockbusting)
- Deny anyone access to or membership in a facility or service (such as a multiple listing service) related to the sale or rental of housing"

Violating the Fair Housing Act is a punishable act and a very serious crime. The civil penalty is up to $10,000. Visit **www.hud.gov** for more information on the Fair Housing Act.

Conclusion

As the real estate industry continues to evolve and change, the concept of For Sale by Owner continues to garner interest as sellers become more advocatory about their homes and their futures. More sellers are realizing not only the monetary benefits to selling on their own, but the relative ease of the entire process — thanks in part to the plethora of information available today for the do-it-yourself type, and the access to resources at the click of a mouse or the turn of a page.

While FSBOs have always represented a significant part of the real estate market in this country, they have been subjected to the natural highs and lows of the real estate industry. The most recent low was the housing market collapse of 2007 to 2009, which forced the market into new and unchartered territory with record foreclosures, short sales, and defaulted mortgages across the country. Some homeowners sold FSBO during this time because they could not afford otherwise, while others took the fate of their future into their own hands during this trying time and successfully sold on their own to save for their future. Those who sold their home on their own saved thousands in a time when every penny counted.

Thankfully, the current housing market — along with the state of the economy on a global scale — remains strong in many areas. FSBOs continue to play an important role. In a thriving seller's market, FSBO remains a popular concept, as many homeowners are confident that the abundance of buyers and increased demand for homes will eliminate, at least in part, the need for a real estate agent to draw in buyers.

The FSBO concept offers flexibility and alternatives, whether in good real estate times or bad. Before you commit to selling FSBO, however, it is important to fully understand and evaluate both the pros *and* cons of selling on your own. Knowledge is power, and the best way to create a successful FSBO experience is to be aware of your specific needs and enlist the appropriate support — whether that be a buyer's agent, an attorney, a discount brokerage, or a marketing strategist — to get your home sold quickly and effectively.

John Henderson of JT Henderson and Associates, a discount brokerage based in Grand Rapids, Michigan, predicts the next decade will bring positive growth for the entire real estate industry. "I think the next ten years will bring changes in this industry no one has even thought of yet. It is an exciting time to be in this business." And you, as a homeowner considering selling, should embrace this shift and tap into all the resources available to you to become your own advocate. With preparation, knowledge, and a little bit of faith, you can become one of the hundreds of thousands of people that successfully sell on their own each year. Good luck!

Glossary

Abnormal sale: A house or property sells for more or less than its current market value — for instance, 25 percent less than comparable homes nearby. Appraisers can ignore abnormal sales when comparing similar properties for value.

Abstract of title: The summarized history of a piece of real estate. It describes each time the property changed hands and notes all encumbrances that have lessened its value or use. This document is certified as complete and truthful by the abstractor.

Acceptance: Completion of a sales contract, when someone offers to buy a property under specific terms and the owner accepts.

Acquisition appraisal: A government agency determines how much to pay a property owner after acquiring their property via negotiation or condemnation.

Acquisition cost: The total price someone pays for a property, with all fees added in.

Actual cash value: The cash value of an improvement for insurance purposes. It equals the cost of replacing something minus the wear and tear.

Addendum: An amendment or revision to a contract both parties consent to and sign.

Adjustable-Rate Mortgage (ARM): Unlike a fixed-rate loan, this home loan has a changing interest rate, which fluctuates to stay current with rates of mortgage loans. It can also change with indexes of the government or financial market.

Affidavit of title: A statement written under oath by a real estate grantor or seller and recognized by a notary public. The person gives his identity, confirms that the title has not changed for the worse since it was last examined, and officially declares that he possesses the property (if appropriate).

Agency disclosure: An agreement most states require: Real estate agents who serve sellers and buyers must disclose whom they are representing.

Agreement of sale: A legal document giving the terms and price of a property sale, which both parties sign.

Appraisal report: The report an appraiser writers describing a property's value and summarizing how it was determined.

Appraised value: The monetary value of a property given in an appraisal report.

Appreciation: The process of a home or property gaining value, which can stem from several factors, including additions to the building, changes in financial markets, and inflation.

"As is" condition: A term in real estate contracts meaning the buyer or renter accepts the property and its flaws just as they are, giving up the right to insist on repairs or renovations.

Asbestos: This mineral, formerly common in insulation and other building materials, is now prohibited because it causes lung disease.

Asking (advertised) price: The amount a property owner hopes a buyer will pay, which may change with negotiation.

Assessed value: The value a tax assessor determines a home to have — used for computing a tax base.

Assessor: A public official responsible for valuing properties for tax purposes.

Associate broker (broker-associates, affiliate brokers, or broker-salespersons): A real estate broker supervised by another broker. This manager holds the associate broker's license.

Attorney's opinion of title: A summarized history of a piece of real estate that an attorney has scrutinized and declared valid, in his opinion.

Backup offer: A second buyer offers to purchase or lease property if the current buyer cannot follow through. When the first buyer backs out, the backup offer takes effect.

Betterment: Any actions improving a piece of real estate.

Bill of sale: This document legally transfers personal property — not real estate title — to a new owner.

Binder: An agreement signifying that a buyer wants to join a real estate contract. The buyer might also make a payment to show earnest desire and ability to purchase the property

Board of Realtors: Licensed real estate professionals belonging to the state and National Association of Realtors.

Breach of contract: Breaking terms of a contract in a legally inexcusable way.

Broker: Someone paid to liaise between sellers and buyers.

Buildable acres: Proportion of land buildings can occupy, considering how much space will go to roads, open areas, setbacks, or spots not suitable for construction.

Building code: Local laws describing how people can use a given property, including what types of construction, building materials, and improvements are legal. Building inspectors make sure people comply.

Buyer's agent: This real estate agent acts on behalf of someone looking to purchase property, and owes that party common-law or statutory agency duties.

Buyer's broker: This broker represents someone looking to buy residential real estate, and owes that party common-law

or statutory agency duties, as a buyer's agent does.

Buyers' market: A situation where buyers can be picky about real estate and shrewd about pricing, because there are more properties than buyers. That happens when economies slow, when too many buildings are constructed, or when population numbers fall.

Cancellation clause: A contract term saying that, if certain things happen, the contract becomes void. For instance, if someone sells property he has been renting out, this clause cancels the lease.

Chain of title: All the times a title has moved from owner to owner, until the present. Attorneys use this history to evaluate the title's status.

Closing: The end of a sale, where buyer pays the seller, both parties or their representatives sign necessary documents, and the buyer receives the title and loan.

Closing costs: Money spent when closing a real estate deal, including fees for appraising property and for the loan and title, but not the actual property.

Closing statement (HUD-1 Settlement Statement): A thorough account of how people spent, gained, and loaned money or started loans, when parties buy and sell real estate.

Commission: Money clients pay brokers for selling or buying property, consisting of a certain percent of the property's price.

Comparable sales (comparables or comps): How much money similar properties nearby sold for — sellers assume another such property in that area will fetch a comparable price.

Concessions: Money or other benefits landlords give tenants to encourage them to sign leases.

Conditional sale: A real estate contract stating that the seller owns the property until the buyer fulfills all the contract's conditions.

Contingency: Circumstances that must exist for a contract to bind the parties. If a contract is contingent on something that never happens, parties are free from it.

Contract: Legal document binding one or both parties involved to fulfill their promises. If a party breaks its promise in the contract, there is a legal remedy.

Conveyance: The document stating that a title passes to a new owner. Also means transference of titles between parties ("closing").

Cosigner: Someone who agrees to pay a debt if the borrower cannot. This party or person signs the loan agreement or promissory note alongside the borrower, but does not own the title or appear on the deed.

Credit: Borrowing money to purchase something valuable and agreeing to repay the lender afterward.

Credit history: A record of someone's debts, past and present, and how reliably the person settled them.

Credit rating: Number describing how much someone deserves a loan, determined from their current finances and credit history.

Credit report: A record of someone's prior residences, jobs, and credit — used to determine if the person is worthy of further credit.

Credit score (credit risk score or FICO score): A calculated summary of the data on someone's credit report.

Creditor: A party owed money.

Curb appeal: A property or home's good looks, as noted by viewers on its street.

Deed: This document legally transfers property to a new owner. That buyer gets the deed after negotiating with and paying the seller.

Department of Housing and Urban Development (HUD): This government agency works to provide clean and safe living spaces without discrimination. It executes plans for community development and federal housing.

Deposit (earnest money): Money one pays when offering to buy a property.

Depreciation: Appraisers use this term to mean lessened value of a property because it grows old, obsolete, or has other defects. For real estate investors, this term means a tax deduction taken while owning income property.

Direct sales comparisons approach (market comparison approach): An appraiser places a value on property by examining the prices on recently purchased estates nearby with similar qualities.

Disclosure: A document listing all the relevant positive and negative information about a piece of real estate.

Discount broker: A broker whose fees are lower than most. These costs might be a flat rate instead of a percentage of the sale.

Dry closing: Both parties have made their agreement, but have not exchanged money or documents. The escrow will finish the closing.

Earnest money: Money a buyer deposits under a contract and loses if he backs out of purchasing the property. But if he buys the real estate, the money goes toward that sale.

Encumbrance: Anything that diminishes a property's worth or makes it less useful or enjoyable. Examples include taxes, mortgages, easements, judgment liens, and rules restricting how the property is used.

Equity: A property's value minus its liabilities, such as unpaid debts

Escrow: Closing of a deal by an escrow agent — a neutral third party. Escrows are also sums of money or valuable possessions passed to a third party, who delivers them when certain conditions are met.

Escrow account (impound account): Used by mortgage lenders and servicing businesses to store money that will pay real estate taxes, homeowner's insurance, and other items.

Escrow agent (escrow company): A third party who neutrally ensures that those having a real estate transaction meet the necessary conditions, such as putting valuables in an escrow account, before any money or property changes hands.

Escrow disbursement: Paying out the money from an escrow account for property expenses due, such as mortgage insurance or taxes.

Estimated closing costs: Approximately how much it costs for a real estate sale to occur.

Ethics: Moral code that guides professional behavior.

Fair Housing Act: Federal legislation stating that someone providing housing cannot discriminate against people because of religion, gender, disability, appearance, race, nationality, or familial status.

Fair market value: Price determined by how much a buyer will agree to pay and how little a seller will accept. In a competitive market, properties would sell at certain times for market value.

Federal Deposit Insurance Corporation (FDIC): An independent part of the U.S. government, this agency insures commercial banks' deposits.

Federal Housing Administration (FHA): This government agency works to make housing available by providing loan programs, as well as guarantee and insurance programs for loans.

Fee appraiser (independent fee appraiser or review appraiser): Someone a prospective property buyer pays to appraise real estate.

FHA loan: Given by a lender approved by the Federal Housing Administration. The FHA insures this loan.

Fixed costs and fixed expenses: Fees that do not change with productivity, sales success, or a property's occupants. Unlike utility bills, which depend on how much water or electricity one uses, fixed costs like fixed-rate mortgage payments remain steady.

Floor plan: Describes how rooms are positioned in a home or other building.

For Sale By Owner (FSBO): An owner sells property without using a real estate broker. This owner works directly with the buyer or the buyer's real estate agent.

Foreclosure: Someone loses property to settle a mortgage debt they cannot pay. This legal procedure turns the property title over to the mortgage lender or it allows a third party to buy the property — without any encumbrances that would lessen its value — in a foreclosure sale.

Full disclosure: Keeping nothing secret that could influence a sale. For example, telling the buyer a property's defects.

GRI: Graduate Realtors Institute. GRIs are people trained in finance, investing, appraisal, law, and sales as prescribed by the Realtors Institute.

Home inspector: A person authorized to assess how operational and structurally sound a property is.

Hazard insurance (homeowner's insurance or fire insurance): Covers property damage by wind, fire, and other destructive forces.

Homeowners' warranty: Insures devices and systems for heating, cooling, and other purposes over a certain period, guaranteeing that they will be fixed if needed.

Department of Housing and Urban Development (HUD): This U.S. government agency manages the Federal Housing Administration and various programs for developing houses and communities.

Improvement: Any construction that boosts a property's value, including private structures like buildings and fences, as well as public structures like roads and water piping.

Inspection report:
A document prepared by a licensed inspector that describes the condition of a property

Insurable title: Can get coverage from title insurance companies.

Inventory: The amount of real estate on the market, not taking into account its quality or availability.

Investment property: Real estate used to earn money.

Land description: Legal account of what a piece of property is like.

Lease: A verbal or written agreement that a tenant will pay for exclusive access to a landlord's property over a certain time period. State laws require long-term leases to be written out, such as agreements exceeding one year.

Lease option/purchase:
Allows a person to rent a home and then apply part of their lease payments toward purchasing it later.

Legal description: An account of what a certain parcel looks like, detailed enough that an independent surveyor could find and recognize it.

Listing agreement: A relationship in which the owner of real estate pays or otherwise compensates a broker to lease or sell property under certain conditions and for a specific price.

Listing broker: The person whose office makes the listing agreement, who can also work directly with the buyer.

Loan-to-value ratio (LTV ratio): Comparison between the sum loaned as a mortgage and the value of the collateral property securing the loan.

Market conditions:
Marketplace traits such as demographics and rates of interest, employment, vacancies, property sales, and leases.

Mortgage: Borrowed money for buying real estate, with the purchased property for collateral.

Mortgage banker: An institution that uses its own funds to make home loans, which mortgage investors and insurance companies can buy.

Mortgage broker: Someone who pairs loan-seekers with mortgage lenders. Brokers are approved to work with certain lenders.

Mortgage commitment: The loan approval from the mortgage company, and it will stipulate any conditions that still need to be cleared in order for borrower to obtain the loan. The contract should stipulate that these conditions be met within seven days of contract acceptance.

Mortgage Insurance (MI): Protects lenders from particular consequences if borrowers fail to repay loans.

Lenders can require mortgage insurance for certain loans.

Mortgage Insurance Premium (MIP): The price of mortgage insurance, paid to private companies or governments.

Multiple listing: Sharing of information and profit between real estate brokers. They agree to give one another details about listings, and to split commissions from the sales.

Multiple listing clause: A clause requiring and authorizing a broker to share a listing he manages with other brokers.

Multiple Listing Service (MLS): A group of brokers who share listing agreements, hoping to find suitable buyers quickly. Acceptable listings include exclusive-agency and exclusive-right-to-sell types.

Nondisclosure: Keeping a fact hidden, whether purposefully or accidentally.

Notary public: Someone who is legally approved to witness and certify that deeds, mortgages, and other contracts or agreements are carried out. A notary public can also give oaths, take affidavits, and perform other duties.

Offer: Stated wish to sell real estate or buy it at a certain cost. Also, this is a selling price for securities or loans.

Offer and acceptance: Needed for a successful real estate sale contract.

Outside of closing (paid outside closing, POC on settlements): Directly paying closing fees without following normal procedures.

Participating broker: Finds a buyer for property listed with a different brokerage firm. Participating brokers can split payment with listing brokers.

Preapproval letter: A lender's opinion that a borrower is eligible for a given loan. Lenders interview possible borrowers, examine their credit histories, and formally evaluate people's finances to decide preapproval.

Prequalified loan: Tells a buyer how much money a lender will loan, based on minimal research on the lender's part.

Preliminary report: Given by a title insurer before the insurance itself, to show that the company is willing to insure a title.

Purchase agreement: Contract giving the conditions and terms of a property sale, signed by both parties.

Purchaser's policy (owner's policy): Insurance the seller provides the buyer as required by their contract. This policy guards against problems with the title.

Qualification: A borrower's eligibility for a loan based on their credit history and ability to repay.

Radon: A natural gas implicated in lung cancer.

Ready, willing, and able buyer: Someone who can and will accept the sales terms a property owner gives, and does what is needed to close the deal.

Real estate agent: Someone with a license to coordinate sales of real property.

Realtor: Registered trademarked name for an active member of the National Association of Realtors.

Repairs: Fixing up features of a property, but not trying to lengthen its useful life as a capital improvement would.

Roof inspection clause: Included in certain sales contracts, it requires the seller to disclose what kind of roofing a home has, and any possible defects. The seller must handle repairs.

Seller carryback: A situation where the party selling the house lends the buyer money to purchase it.

Seller's market: Occurs when demand for real estate rises or supply drops, allowing sellers to charge more.

Selling broker: Real estate licensee who locates a buyer.

Short sale: Occurs when an owner sells property but the proceeds do not pay off his mortgage. The lender lets the remaining debt go, opting for less money and avoiding a foreclosure.

Special conditions (contingencies): Must be fulfilled before the real estate contract containing them can bind parties involved.

Staging: A scaffold that supports construction materials and workers, removed when no longer needed. Staging is also an informal term for getting homes ready to impress potential buyers.

Subprime loan: A loan with elevated fees and interest, given to someone with a lower credit score.

Termite inspection: A professional check for signs of invading termites. Loans backed by the FHA necessitate these inspections, and real estate contracts might suggest them.

Title: Ownership of real estate, or proof thereof.

Title company: A company that insures titles and resolves who owns them.

Title exam: Investigation verifying that a seller's ownership of property appears in public records. It reveals any encumbrances the property bears.

Title insurance: It protects property buyers against flaws or legal problems that come with their real estate, if the policy mentions them.

Title report: An early description of a title, not including its ownership history.

Title search: A search of public records to reveal any potential problems that might hinder passing property to a new owner.

Transfer tax: Taken by state or federal officials when real estate changes hands.

Under contract: When a seller is under contract, it means he is committed to the transaction with a certain buyer and unable to choose another.

VA loan: Made through a lender authorized by the Department of Veterans Affairs. A VA loan provides a safe way for financing veterans who qualify.

Value-added: The worth a property is expected to gain after improvement or repair.

Walkthrough: A visit to a home by the buyer just before closing the deal. The buyer makes sure the property is unoccupied and free from unexpected defects.

Warranty deed: Guarantees that the person giving the

deed will guard the recipient against all possible claims.

Water rights: Possessed by people living on bodies of water, these rights describe how owners can and cannot use nearby water sources.

Wear and tear: Weathering of property from the elements, its age, or from people using it.

Zoning: Dividing cities or towns into areas meant for different kinds of buildings or uses, which laws and regulations dictate.

Works Cited

Brown, Ray; Tyson, Eric. *House Selling for Dummies.* Indiana: Wiley Publishing, Inc. 2008.

Bunton, David S. "The Boom and the Bust of the U.S. Real Estate Market: What Went Wrong and the Lessons We Learned." October, 2008. **www.appraisalfoundation.org,** September 26, 2009.

Carlyle, Erin. Forbes, "Bidding Wars For Homes Have Become The New Normal In Many U.S. Cities," **www.forbes.com,** April 13, 2016.

Christie, Les. "Foreclosures: Worst Three Months of All Time," October 15, 2009. **http://money.cnn.com,** October 17, 2009.

Dedman, Bill. "Recession Ends in 79 Metro Areas, Index Shows," October 15, 2009. **www.msnbc.msn.com,** October 17, 2009.

Department of Housing and Urban Development. "Fair Housing Laws and Presidential Executive Orders," October 15, 2009. **www.hud.gov**, October 20, 2009.

Energy Star®. "Energy Star® at Home and at Work," **www.energystar.gov**, October 19, 2009.

Gopalakrishnan, Jessica. HomeGain 2009 Top 12 Home Improvements Survey Results," November 4, 2009. **http://blog.homegain.com**, November 8, 2009.

Irwin, Robert. *For Sale by Owner*. New York: Kaplan Publishing, 2008.

Lending Tree. "The Best Time to Sell Your Home," August 6, 2007. **www.lendingtree.com**, October 17, 2009.

Lynch, Sarah. "Best Cities to Buy A Home," June 22, 2009, Forbes Magazine. **www.forbes.com**, October 12, 2009.

McLaughlin, Ralph. "House Arrest: How Low Inventory Is Slowing Home Buying," March 21, 2016.

National Association of Realtors. "Field Guide to Quick Real Estate Statistics," September 2009. **www.realtor.org**, October 17, 2009.

National Association of Realtors. "NAR: Real Estate Resources: 2009 Code of Ethics and Standards of Practice," **www.realtor.org**, October 28, 2009.

Nichole, Piper. *The For Sale by Owner Handbook*. New Jersey: Career Press, 2005.

RealtyTrac. "Columbia, SC, Real Estate Trends," **www.realtytrac.com**, October 16, 2009.

Stegemoeller, Ingrid. "Tri-City Homes in Short Supply," June 24, 2009, Tri-City Herald. **www.tri-cityherald.com**, September 15, 2009.

U.S. Securities and Exchanges Commission, **www.sec.gov**, October 13, 2009.

Woodall, Charles. "Home Seller Series: 3 Types of Homebuyers You Need to Know About," March 4, 2009. **http://dothanhomesearch.com**, October 17, 2009.

Woolsey, Matt. "Where Home Prices Are Likely to Rise." August 25, 2008, Forbes Magazine. **www.forbes.com**, October 12, 2009.

Woolsey, Matt. "America's Next Foreclosure Capitals," October 20, 2008, Forbes Magazine. **www.forbes.com**, October 12, 2009.

About the Author

Jackie Bondanza is a developmental book editor and a freelance writer. She has written about real estate, education, entertainment, travel, health, and lifestyle for iVillage, MSN, *Online Degrees Magazine, Hemispheres Magazine, Southern California Senior Life, Northridge Magazine,* and *College Bound Teen Magazine.* She has a master's degree in journalism and has written copy for both television and radio. She has also appeared as an education and lifestyle consultant for a variety of national television programs.

As a developmental editor, Jackie works with authors to develop books ranging in genre from historical non-fiction and reference to pop culture and literature. In addition to her editorial work, Jackie writes a blog on international aid issues for Globalhood, an international consulting firm, and she also leads workshops for homeless writers around the country. She currently lives in New York City with her husband and her dog. Visit her at **www.JackieBondanza.com**.

Index

U.S. Department of Housing and Urban Development (HUD): 220

Victorian: 179

Word-of-mouth: 9, 192